W9-BEG-929

THE

Responsive Classroom®
Assessment Tool
for Teachers

© 2012 by Northeast Foundation for Children, Inc.
© 2015 by Center for Responsive Schools, Inc.

All rights reserved. Assessment forms on pages 67–123 may be photocopied
for educators' use. No other part of this tool may be reproduced in any form
or by any electronic or mechanical means, including information storage and
retrieval systems, without permission in writing from the publisher.

ISBN: 978-1-892989-51-2

Cover photographs (clockwise from left) © Peter Wrenn, Alice Proujansky,
and Jeff Woodward. All rights reserved.

Icons © Lynn Zimmerman. All rights reserved.

Design by Helen Merena

Center for Responsive Schools, Inc.
85 Avenue A, P.O. Box 718
Turners Falls, MA 01376-0718

800-360-6332   www.responsiveclassroom.org

Fifth printing 2015

Printed on recycled paper

Table of Contents

THE GUIDE

THE TOOL

Introduction

*"A lot of people notice when you succeed,
but they don't see what it takes to get there."*

Dawn Staley, WNBA basketball player

Implementing *Responsive Classroom®* principles and practices to the fullest takes time and effort. Sustaining that effort, like any learning endeavor, requires teachers to set goals, work on those goals, reflect and evaluate their progress, and then set new goals to begin the learning process anew. Teachers need considerable support and specific feedback as they engage in this learning process.

This assessment tool is one source of such support. It's intended to help teachers deepen their understanding of *Responsive Classroom* practices and engage in meaningful reflection about teaching and learning.

This process of reflection and assessment, when approached with genuine curiosity and openness, will ultimately strengthen teaching practices and enhance the learning of adults and children in schools. *The Responsive Classroom Assessment Tool for Teachers* provides users with data to substantiate areas of strength and challenge, and action steps that provide clear directions for future growth. Both are necessary to make real and lasting changes in teaching practices.

This guide explains how to use the tool to its fullest potential. It offers teachers information about who can benefit from the tool as well as comprehensive instructions on how to use it. Detailed examples of how different teachers have used it are offered along with strategies and resources for improving specific *Responsive Classroom* practices.

What Is *The Responsive Classroom Assessment Tool for Teachers?*

The Responsive Classroom Assessment Tool for Teachers is a rating system consisting of 125 specific aspects of *Responsive Classroom* practice on which teachers can be evaluated. The items are organized in eight sections:

Section 1: Arrival Time

Section 2: Interactive Modeling

Section 3: Morning Meeting

Section 4: Guided Discovery

Section 5: Academic Choice

Section 6: Classroom Organization

Section 7: Classroom Management and Teacher Language

Section 8: Working With Families

For each item included in these sections, the assessment tool provides specific and concrete examples of how a teacher's practice might look at three different levels of *Responsive Classroom* implementation:

■ A beginning level at which teachers recognize that their implementation needs work

■ A middle level at which teachers are making good progress but still have some areas for growth

■ A higher level at which teachers feel that their practice is strong but needs refinements at a very sophisticated and complex level

For instance, item "MM1" addresses whether teachers are providing an adequate space for Morning Meeting:

MM 1 **Space** In our Morning Meetings ...	**1**	**3**	**5**
	... *few* students have room to sit comfortably in a circle/oval and view everyone and everything.	... *most* students have room to sit comfortably in a circle/oval and view everyone and everything.	... *all* students have room to sit comfortably in a circle/oval and view everyone and everything.

The "1" rating indicates to teachers that there are some problems with their implementation of this item—that children need more room to sit comfortably and should be able to see everyone and everything. This observation can lead teachers to reflect on the possibility that children who are not comfortable or who cannot see may be less engaged and/or less likely to model desired behavior. Teachers giving themselves the "3" rating know that they are meeting most students' needs but still might need to pay more attention to ensuring that all, not just most, students can sit comfortably and see everyone and everything.

Teachers at the highest rating level of "5" know that they have provided adequate space for Morning Meetings. They can then think about space issues at a higher level: Are students choosing to sit next to the same friends all the time? Is the space being used at other times of the day to maximize instruction? Are instructional supplies, like an easel, markers, and books, easily accessible to the teacher? By providing concrete examples of what implementation looks like at each level, the assessment tool gives teachers a practical idea of how they are doing with a given aspect of their *Responsive Classroom* practice, and it gives specific information about what they might change in order to improve.

In addition to looking at information about a specific aspect of practice, a teacher can come up with an overall rating for a larger area of *Responsive Classroom* practice. For instance, MM1, the item referring to space for Morning Meetings, is part of the Morning Meeting section. A teacher can assess her progress on MM1 and all of the other Morning Meeting items to come up with a global score for how she is developing with Morning Meeting practice as a whole.

Some teachers may want to use all 125 items to assess their complete *Responsive Classroom* practice. This provides an assessment of their overall *Responsive Classroom* implementation.

Although the assessment tool relies on a numerical rating system to build some objectivity into the process of evaluation, the goal of the assessment tool is not to obtain a particular score. Rather, as discussed in the next section, the primary purpose of the tool is to spark reflection and growth in *Responsive Classroom* practice and ultimately to lead to better teaching and learning.

Who Should Use
This Assessment Tool?

Three different groups of teachers and educators can benefit from using *The Responsive Classroom Assessment Tool for Teachers*:

A. Classroom teachers

B. Special area teachers

C. Teams of teachers

Each of these groups has unique needs and concerns, which are addressed beginning on page 7.

The assessment tool can provide teachers with the kind of feedback and support that is frequently missing in schools today. Teachers are often trained in practices like the *Responsive Classroom* approach and then go back to their classrooms alone or with just a few colleagues to try to implement what they have learned. They receive little feedback to know whether they are implementing what they have learned "correctly" or to keep up the momentum and excitement they may have felt immediately after the initial training. Even teachers who stay enthusiastic about the *Responsive Classroom* approach after initial training and who complete advanced training may forget some aspects of what they learned and wonder whether they are implementing practices in the spirit and manner in which they were intended.

The assessment tool can help all of these teachers to reflect, think deeply, and continue growing in *Responsive Classroom* implementation. Whether a teacher has been using *Responsive Classroom* practices for two years or for twenty years, there is always more to know and understand. The assessment tool is one way of stimulating that knowledge and understanding.

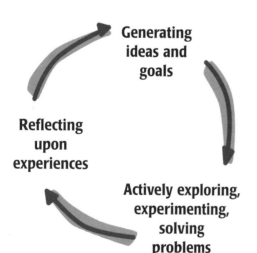

Adults learn best, just as children do, when they are engaged in a natural learning cycle that includes goal-setting, exploration, and reflection. The assessment tool helps launch teachers into this cycle. Teachers begin by generating a learning goal that specifies the aspect(s) of their practice on which they want to focus. They then enter the exploration phase by using the assessment tool to rate themselves with regard to the identified aspect(s) of their practice. Next, they reflect on the results—their strengths and areas for improvement.

The assessment tool encourages teachers to use the results of the assessment to specify areas for growth, set new goals, and use strategies and resources listed in the guide to improve in those areas. In this way, they begin the learning cycle again. Whether a teacher is experienced or a novice at implementing *Responsive Classroom* practices, the goal of the assessment process is always further learning.

The assessment tool was created for teachers at all stages in their *Responsive Classroom* implementation and teaching careers. Any classroom or special area teacher or any teaching team trying to implement one or more aspects of the *Responsive Classroom* approach can benefit from it. Teachers or teams might use the assessment tool to:

- Assess their practice for themselves and their own professional growth. Teachers who might want to embark on this path could fall into any of these categories:

  → Teachers who feel comfortable and confident with their *Responsive Classroom* practice but want an objective way to look at that practice and think about ways to elevate it.

  → Teachers who have sensed problems with their implementation but need help figuring out what the particular problems and their causes are.

  → Teachers who have taken *Responsive Classroom* coursework or read *Responsive Classroom* materials some time ago and are beginning to feel "stuck" in familiar routines. They may want to use the assessment tool to inspire new thinking about their practice and to find new directions.

  → Teachers who have an interest in a particular *Responsive Classroom* practice, such as Guided Discovery, and want to conduct some self-study concerning that practice.

  → Teachers who have intentionally begun their *Responsive Classroom* work by undertaking only one or two *Responsive Classroom* teaching practices. They may want to evaluate their implementation of these practices before moving forward and adding new *Responsive Classroom* teaching practices.

- Examine the effectiveness of their *Responsive Classroom* practice more formally as part of their ongoing professional growth and development plans. These teachers may make more public use of the assessment tool, as they use it to document for their administrators or district leaders how they have progressed with regard to identified teaching goals.

A FLEXIBLE TOOL

The Responsive Classroom Assessment Tool for Teachers is a flexible tool that can be administered and used in several ways. All have different strengths and emphases and serve different purposes.

A teacher can assess herself.

A teacher can easily use the assessment tool to assess her own practice. The tool was initially designed to facilitate self-evaluation and reflection, which is why the "I" voice is used.

A colleague can assess a colleague.

For many reasons, a teacher might also ask a colleague to observe her practice using the assessment tool. Having another party observe her practice might help to point out strengths or areas for growth that the teacher might not have noticed on her own. In addition, a colleague can apply the tool in "real time," that is, as a teacher is teaching. Having a colleague do the observation also gives the teacher someone with whom to confer as she moves into the reflection phase of the learning process.

A teacher can use a combination of approaches.

A teacher might be most comfortable self-assessing at first and then inviting a colleague into her classroom to gain another view of her practice. Or, a teacher might simultaneously complete the assessment herself and have a colleague observe and complete the assessment. Such a dual rating would give the teacher more information on which to base decisions and set goals.

How to Use This Assessment Tool, With Examples

Specific information follows that applies to each group that can benefit from using the assessment tool.

FOR CLASSROOM TEACHERS

Generating Ideas and Goals: Establishing Purposes and Choosing Appropriate Sections of the Assessment Tool

To begin the natural learning cycle, teachers should think about how they will use the tool to help them meet their goals:

- Some teachers might want to do all of the assessment at once or in several closely spaced sessions to obtain a complete picture of their overall *Responsive Classroom* practice. For instance, they might evaluate themselves on "Arrival Time" and "Morning Meeting" one day and then follow up the next day by assessing their use of "Interactive Modeling" and "Guided Discovery." They could continue on this path until they have completed the entire evaluation.

- Other teachers might consider assessing themselves on only one or two components at a time. They might choose to begin with what they think are areas of relative strength and then use the assessment tool to identify whether their perceptions are accurate. They might reflect on how they can refine those areas of strength even further and then slowly look at other areas of implementation as they are ready for them. Or, they might want to begin with a problematic area and use the assessment tool to help them target why that area seems troublesome and how to improve it.

Teachers also need to decide whether to engage in pre-assessment reflection and reading or just begin the assessment process with no preparation:

- Some teachers may prefer to have their first use of the assessment tool occur "cold" with no preparation or reflection. These teachers will simply identify the area of practice on which they want to focus and begin to rate themselves on the various items within this area. They might feel that such a stark initial assessment gives the most accurate view of their practice.

- Other teachers may be interested in some pre-assessment reflection exercises (provided at the beginning of each section of the tool). These exercises will help teachers think about what they already know about a particular topic, identify questions that they may have, and set the stage for deeper reflection about what they discover through the assessment process.

■ Some teachers might also want to review relevant resources (a variety of which are included on pages 38–63) before they assess themselves on their implementation. This could make the assessment process richer for some teachers.

 Actively Exploring, Experimenting, and Solving Problems: Administering the Assessment Tool

To use the instrument itself, teachers should follow these steps:

1 Read each item carefully to be sure you understand which aspect of your practice you are assessing. If you are observing another teacher, be sure to read each item beforehand to make sure you understand exactly what you will be looking for as you observe.

2 For each item, circle the rating (the number 1, 3, or 5) that best describes the item being observed. If you cannot decide between two ratings, mark the lower number. The mere fact of uncertainty indicates that this item may be one that needs further effort. Do not be concerned if the ratings are not all 5's for any particular section or for the whole assessment process. The assessment tool is designed to present a range of implementation with 5 often representing the ideal. Most teachers, even those who have been using *Responsive Classroom* practices well for long periods of time, will have areas in which they find room for improvement.

3 After completing an entire section, calculate the average score for the section:

■ Add up the total points for that section.

■ Divide that number by the number of items in that section. Any item that is not answered (for instance, because this practice is not used) should be scored as a zero and the zero should be calculated into the average score. There are a few items that can be scored as nonapplicable (n/a). Do not use these items to calculate the average score.

4 Look at the average scores and determine what they mean for you:

An average of …	Indicates that …
4.0 or above	Your implementation is strong
3.0–3.9	You are making good progress
Less than 3.0	You need to strengthen your implementation

5 If you are working on completing all eight sections, when you have done so, complete the final summary page included with the assessment tool. This will give you an overall picture of your current *Responsive Classroom* practice.

Reflecting Upon Experiences: Using the Results to Form an Action Plan

Getting a rating with the assessment tool is just one step in the learning process. Some teachers may want to complete the reflection questions included at the end of each section before moving on to another section. These questions are designed to help teachers set some goals for further learning and refinement related to the component or practice they are assessing. Teachers may also want to reflect more generally and form an action plan as to what the next steps in the learning process will be. They may want to formulate a plan of improvement using some of the ideas and resources contained on pages 38–63 of this guide.

EXAMPLE:

How Mrs. Garcia used the assessment tool as a classroom teacher

Mrs. Garcia became interested in the *Responsive Classroom* approach by taking the Responsive Classroom Sampler, a one-day introductory workshop. She then followed up her interest by reading much of *The Morning Meeting Book* and then taking the four-day Responsive Classroom Course. She has been trying to implement several key *Responsive Classroom* teaching practices: Morning Meeting, creating rules, Interactive Modeling, teacher language, and logical consequences. She is interested in assessing herself in each of these areas because she was very motivated by the training she received and does not want to let the momentum from that training die out.

Generating Ideas and Goals: Establishing Purposes and Choosing Appropriate Sections of the Assessment Tool

Mrs. Garcia's main purpose in using the assessment tool is to explore ideas and spark her own professional growth. She decides to begin the assessment process with the area in which she believes she is strongest, Section 3: Morning Meeting.

She begins the process by reflecting on her current Morning Meeting practice using the pre-assessment reflection questions, shown as follows:

I. Reflect on what you currently know about the area of practice you are planning to assess.

—Morning Meeting has 4 parts: greeting, sharing, group activity, and morning message.

—It should happen first thing in the morning in a circle, and all students should attend.

—It should build cooperation and should not include competitive games or language.

—You can incorporate academics into the meeting by using them in your message.

—You should scaffold the skills you are teaching students at Morning Meeting.

II. Thoroughly read through this section of the assessment. Note ideas that confirm your best understanding of this practice and ideas that raise questions for you. Think about what the most important goals of this practice are.

In looking through the section, I think that most of my current knowledge was correct!

The purposes of Morning Meeting are to develop a strong classroom community, for students to feel as if they are part of the group, and for all of us to get to know each other.

Questions I now have:

—What is Interactive Modeling? How is it different from other kinds of modeling?

—Is sharing more complicated than I thought?

—Am I supposed to incorporate academics in other parts of the meeting? How will I do this?

III. If you have many questions or potential misunderstandings about this practice, you may want to refer to some of the resources listed in the guide before you assess yourself with the assessment tool.

IV. Complete the section assessment.

 Actively Exploring, Experimenting, and Solving Problems: Administering the Assessment Tool

After reviewing her answers and reflecting, Mrs. Garcia then administers Section 3: Morning Meeting. The ratings she gives herself are shown below:

G E N E R A L

	1	**3**	**5**
MM 1 **Space** In our Morning Meetings . . .	. . . *few* students have room to sit comfortably in a circle/oval and view everyone and everything.	. . . *most* students have room to sit comfortably in a circle/oval and view everyone and everything.	. . . *all* students have room to sit comfortably in a circle/oval and view everyone and everything.
MM 2 **Transition to Meeting** When it's time for Morning Meeting to begin . . .	. . . *few* students come quickly, quietly, and empty-handed on most days.	. . . *many* students come quickly, quietly, and empty-handed on most days.	. . . *most* students come quickly, quietly, and empty-handed on most days.
MM 3 **Processes** During many Morning Meetings, students respond to my designation of our greeting, sharing, and/or group activity with . . .	. . . an *extended* amount of negotiation or complaining.	. . . a *moderate* amount of negotiation or complaining.	. . . *little or no* negotiation or complaining.

(In MM 1, the **3** is circled; in MM 2, the **3** is circled; in MM 3, the **5** is circled.)

	1	**③**	**5**
MM 4 **Academic Content of the Four Components** (Greeting, Sharing, Group Activity, Morning Message) In our Morning Meetings ...	... usually *no* components incorporate academic content directly related to our curriculum or student needs.	... usually *one* component incorporates academic content directly related to our curriculum or student needs.	... usually *two or more* components incorporate academic content directly related to our curriculum or student needs in a fun way that builds community.
MM 5 **Length** Morning Meetings in our class ...	... *frequently* last less than twenty minutes or more than thirty minutes.	... *sometimes* last approximately twenty to thirty minutes.	... *usually* last approximately twenty to thirty minutes. ⑤
MM 6 **Order** Morning Meetings in our class ...	... *usually do not* follow the order of (1) greeting, (2) sharing, (3) group activity, and (4) morning message.	... *sometimes do* follow the order of (1) greeting, (2) sharing, (3) group activity, and (4) morning message.	... *usually do* follow the order of (1) greeting, (2) sharing, (3) group activity, and (4) morning message. ⑤
MM 7 **Student Participation** During our Morning Meetings ...	... *many* students leave for breaks, errands, or previously scheduled tasks or sessions.	... *most* students remain (that is, only one or two students leave the meeting for breaks, errands, or previously scheduled sessions).	... *all* students usually remain (that is, students rarely miss Morning Meeting for any reason). ⑤

MM 8 **Teaching Greetings** In general, before the class does a greeting, I ...	**1** ... *do not* usually use Interactive Modeling to teach or remind children about expectations for behavior during the greeting (Interactive Modeling consists of the teacher and one or more students demonstrating expected behavior, students identifying key behaviors, and all students practicing).	**3** ... *sometimes* use Interactive Modeling to teach and review appropriate behavior during the greeting or *regularly* use portions of Interactive Modeling (Interactive Modeling consists of the teacher and one or more students demonstrating expected behavior, students identifying key behaviors, and all students practicing).	**5** ... *regularly* use Interactive Modeling to teach and review appropriate behavior during the greeting (Interactive Modeling consists of the teacher and one or more students demonstrating expected behavior, students identifying key behaviors, and all students practicing).
MM 9 **Participation** Most of the time in our Morning Meetings ...	**1** ... not all students are greeted by class members.	**3** ... each student is greeted and also greets at least one other class member.	**(5)** ... everyone in the classroom (including all adults, visitors, etc.) is greeted and also greets at least one other person.

MM 10 **Appropriateness** Generally, during our Morning Meetings ...	**1** ... *most* students' sharing is focused on games, toys, possessions, or inappropriate personal experiences.	**(3)** ... *most* students' sharing is focused on appropriate personal experiences, relationships, or ideas and items related to the social or academic curriculum.	**5** ... *all* students' sharing is focused on appropriate personal experiences, relationships, or ideas and items related to the social or academic curriculum.
MM 11 **Appropriateness** During Morning Meeting, students ...	**1** ... *often* share information that may be hurtful or embarrassing to others.	**(3)** ... *often* share information that is respectful of others and does not lead to hurt feelings.	**5** ... *always or almost always* share information that is respectful of others and does not lead to hurt feelings.

	1	**3**	**5**
MM 12 **Sharing Focus** Generally, during sharing …	… *few* students' sharings are focused on one main idea with a few supporting details.	… *many* students' sharings are focused on one main idea with a few supporting details.	… *all or almost all* students' sharings are focused on one main idea with a few supporting details.
MM 13 **Speaking Skills** Generally, during sharing …	… *many* students look down, away, or only at the teacher as they share.	… *many* students look around at all the others in the circle as they share.	… *all or almost all* students look around at all the others in the circle as they share.
MM 14 **Speaking Skills** In general …	… *many* students who share speak too softly or unclearly to be understood.	… *many* students who share speak loudly and clearly enough to be understood.	… *all or almost all* students who share speak loudly and clearly enough to be understood.
MM 15 **Sharing Length** Generally, during our dialogue sharing …	… *many* students limit their sharing to one sentence (for example, "I went on a fun trip") or expand their sharing into overly long narrations.	… *some* students provide enough information (that is, several sentences) to give listeners important details, but not so much as to make sharing overly long.	… *many or most* students provide enough information (that is, several sentences) to provide listeners with important details, but not so much as to make sharing overly long.
MM 16 **Questions and Comments** Generally, during dialogue sharing …	… *no* questions or comments are asked for or given.	… I ask or tell the group to offer questions or comments and/or *some* sharers receive questions or comments.	… *most or all* sharing students tell the group they are ready for questions and comments and all sharing students receive at least two or three questions or comments.

MM 17 **Questions and Comments** The questions and comments students offer are ...	**1** ... *frequently* not respect-ful of the sharer and/or are off topic.	**(3)** ... *often* respectful of the sharer and on topic.	**5** ... *almost always* respectful of the sharer and on topic.

GROUP ACTIVITY

MM 18 **Teaching Activities** In general, I ...	**(1)** ... *do not* usually use Interactive Modeling to teach or remind children about expectations for behavior during the group activity (Interactive Model-ing consists of the teacher and one or more students demonstrating expected behavior, students identify-ing key behaviors, and all students practicing).	**3** ... *sometimes* use Interactive Modeling to teach and review appropriate behavior during the group activity or regularly use portions of Interactive Modeling (Interactive Model-ing consists of the teacher and one or more students demonstrating expected behavior, students identify-ing key behaviors, and all students practicing).	**5** ... *regularly* use Interactive Modeling to teach and review appropriate behavior during the group activity (Interactive Modeling con-sists of the teacher and one or more students demon-strating expected behavior, students identifying key behaviors, and all students practicing).
MM 19 **Community-Building** In general, the activities I choose encourage ...	**1** ... divisiveness and/or competitiveness in the group. *For example, I choose elimi-nation games.*	**(3)** ... student cooperation, but students often do not help each other and/or make the activities into a competition.	**5** ... student cooperation and community spirit. *For example, I choose coopera-tive games in which students help one another.*

MORNING MESSAGE

MM 20 **Preparation** In general, I ...	**1** ... *often do not* write a morning message.	**3** ... *often* write the morning message after students have arrived.	**(5)** ... *usually* write the morning message before students arrive.

MM 21 **Formatting** The morning message ...	**1** ... is *rarely* written on chart paper and displayed at children's eye level.	**3** ... is *sometimes* written on chart paper and displayed at children's eye level.	**(5)** ... is *always or almost always* written on chart paper and displayed at children's eye level.
MM 22 **Location** The morning message ...	**1** ... is *not* located in an easily accessible area of the room (that is, approximately three to five students cannot get close to the message); instead, it's in a tight corner, behind my desk, etc.	**3** ... is *sometimes* located in an easily accessible area of the room (that is, where approximately three to five students can easily get close to the message).	**(5)** ... is *regularly* located in an easily accessible area of the room (that is, where approximately three to five students can easily get close to the message).
MM 23 **Readability** Usually, the morning message ...	**1** ... focuses on multiple topics, and may use several words or concepts that several students find difficult.	**(3)** ... uses vocabulary and academic content familiar to *most* students or focuses primarily on one topic.	**5** ... uses vocabulary and academic content familiar to *all or almost all* students and focuses primarily on one topic.
MM 24 **Interactivity** In general, the morning message ...	**1** ... does not include a component that inspires students to contribute their ideas.	**(3)** .... inspires students to contribute their ideas but only by writing or drawing on the message.	**5** ... inspires students to contribute their ideas in various ways. *For example, the students can contribute by writing or drawing on the message, considering "thinking questions" that we discuss during the meeting, and/or sharing related ideas during the meeting.*

MM 25 **Engagement** In general, prior to the start of Morning Meeting ...	1 ... *many* students need a lot of prompting to read the morning message and/or need reminders to follow directions found in the message.	③ ... *many* students read the morning message with little prompting and follow directions found in the message.	5 ... *all or almost all* students read the morning message with little prompting and follow directions found in the message.
MM 26 **Usage** In general, during Morning Meeting I ...	1 ... *rarely* have the whole class read/discuss the morning message as a way to transition to the academic content of the day.	③ ... *sometimes* have the whole class read/discuss the morning message as a way to transition to the academic content of the day.	5 ... *always or almost always* have the whole class read/discuss the morning message as a way to transition to the academic content of the day.

Morning Meeting   Total number of points* = _92_ divided by 26 items = _3.5_ (average)

Note: Items that you do not rate should be assigned a point value of zero.

Mrs. Garcia counts the total number of points she has given herself as 92. She divides that by 26, the total number of items in the Morning Meeting section, to get an average score of 3.5. On the basis of her score and the guidelines given for using the assessment tool, Mrs. Garcia decides she is making good progress with regard to Morning Meeting. She wants to delve more deeply and look at both what is going well and how she could improve her Morning Meetings.

 Reflecting Upon Experiences: Using the Results to Form an Action Plan

She then answers the post-assessment reflection questions below:

Mrs. Garcia's Post-Assessment Reflection

Average score _3.5_   Strength area: Good progress: Area to be improved:
                         (average: 4.0 or more)   *(average: 3.0–3.9)*   *(average: less than 3.0)*

1. What is an area of particular strength with this practice? What has contributed to your success?

—I've got the basics. My meetings are the right length and I do things in the right order. Students are getting to know each other.

—I'm meeting the basic purposes of greeting. Students feel happier beginning the day with someone greeting them in a kind and friendly way. They feel like they belong.

—I'm on target with morning message. I do them ahead of time and put them in a place where kids can easily read and work with them. Kids are excited to read the message. I'm pretty good about sticking to one topic and I make sure there's an interactive piece.

—I got high scores for student engagement! I thought that students were energized and participating fully and it's great to have that affirmed. How can I keep this going throughout the day?

—I think I've been successful with my Morning Meetings because I immediately saw the benefit of doing them. And I really enjoy the meetings myself, which keeps me motivated to keep improving them.

2. What would you identify as areas for improvement?

—Space for my meeting. I really need to think about how I set up the space for the meeting. Right now, I've got more of an amoeba than a circle. This means some kids have trouble seeing and being seen and might feel like they're not part of the meeting. I wonder if this is why there are some behavior issues?

—Interactive Modeling. I know I've been confused about the differences between the ways I've always done modeling and Interactive Modeling. I'd like to learn more.

—Sharing. I wonder if I'm shortchanging kids in this area. I've just let them share without paying attention to whether they're looking at classmates or summarizing or using a loud enough voice. I want to think about how I *can teach these skills. Maybe sharing could be a time to focus on public speaking.*

—Academics. I've been choosing what to do in meeting based on how I'm feeling when I do my lesson planning rather than really thinking about how to tie things in with the curriculum. I mostly think about academics when I write my message. Maybe I could bring academics into other parts of the meeting?

3. Prioritize these areas for improvement in order of most importance to you.

—I think I will keep them in the order I listed them for my priorities. I am especially interested in focusing on classroom organization first.

4. For your first area of priority, create a self-improvement plan (use notes page if needed). See suggestions in the strategies and resources section for specific ideas about ways to work on one or more of the components of this practice.

5. Continue this process with other priority areas.

6. When will you assess this practice again?

—I will look at Morning Meeting again after I have worked my way through all my areas for improvement.

In her post-assessment reflection, Mrs. Garcia identifies several areas in which she believes she is relatively strong:

- Morning Meeting basics
- Greeting
- Morning message
- Overall student engagement/participation

She also realizes there are several areas about which she had some confusion from her initial training or that she wants to explore further:

- *Space for Morning Meeting:* Mrs. Garcia had not really spent much time thinking about her circle space since she first taught her children to make a circle after attending the *Responsive Classroom* one-day workshop. She realizes that her circle is more like an amoeba and that there are always one or two students who seem to get squeezed out. Children often complain that they are not able to see. She begins to wonder about whether some of the minor behavioral issues she sees during Morning Meeting could be arising from the circle arrangement.

■ *Use of Interactive Modeling:* Mrs. Garcia has difficulty marking herself on the use of Interactive Modeling for greetings and activities because she is not sure that she understands the difference between Interactive Modeling and modeling. She thinks she models, but she is not sure, so she decides to give herself the lower rating and investigate this issue more at a later time.

■ *Sharing:* After looking at the various items addressing the sharing component of her Morning Meetings, Mrs. Garcia begins to wonder whether the sharers are performing to their full capability and whether this component is meeting its purposes fully. She also wonders whether she has been explicit enough about what sharing should look like and about teaching the skills needed for productive sharing. For instance, she does not think she has taught the sharers to look around the circle and make eye contact with everyone. She is also not sure that she has sufficiently taught the class about the importance of having clear summaries and speaking at a high enough volume.

■ *Academics:* Mrs. Garcia realizes that she often chooses greetings, sharing topics, and activities somewhat randomly. She wonders whether she could be more purposeful in this area and particularly whether she could incorporate academics more fully.

Mrs. Garcia decides to tackle these issues one at a time. She formulates a plan for each. She begins by thinking more deeply about her space for Morning Meeting and uses some of the strategies and resources suggested in the guide to help with her exploration. She takes the following steps:

■ She decides to look at *Classroom Spaces That Work* and reads the section about making space for a meeting circle (pages 61–75). On the basis of her reading, she formulates several new ideas for the circle space:

→ She wonders whether she could use the circle effectively for other types of instruction. Right now she primarily uses it for class meetings and read-alouds, but she thinks her students might benefit if she used it even more frequently.

→ She thinks she needs more room for the circle and thinks about furniture she can move or remove to make the circle larger.

→ She likes the suggestion in the book about more specifically delineating where each child sits in the circle by marking spots on the rug with tape. She is excited to think that this simple step could easily reduce questions or arguments about where everyone should be and how all of her students can fit.

- Mrs. Garcia invites a colleague, Ms. Ackerman, into her room because she has always liked the layout of Ms. Ackerman's room and suspects that arranging classroom space may be a strength of Ms. Ackerman's. She asks Ms. Ackerman to come in and consider ways to enlarge the circle area. Together, they make the following decisions:

  → They regroup the students' desks from their previous formation—two long rows of desks facing each other—to small groups of four or five desks around the room.

  → They remove a table Mrs. Garcia sometimes used in the back to set out materials for art or science projects. Mrs. Garcia is sad to see a piece of furniture leave, but she feels that the table was taking up too much room and was not being used effectively. She plans to use the top of a nearby bookshelf or her back counter when she needs to set out supplies.

  → They outline a perfect circle with enough spots for everyone by first laying down picture books to approximate the size of each child's seat and leaving approximately three to four inches between each book. They then mark the spaces with a small piece of tape.

After taking these simple steps, Mrs. Garcia is pleased to find that all of the children have a spot in the circle, can see everyone and everything, and are much less likely to argue or have small issues about where to sit or whether they can see. She is excited about the difference this change quickly makes in her Morning Meetings and the rest of her day. She also has begun to have the students meet in the circle for mini-lessons and closing reflections and at other times of the day. The process of changing her circle takes about one and a half weeks.

Inspired by her success in this area, Mrs. Garcia moves on to the other areas of Morning Meeting she identified in the assessment. She spends about a month on the issue of Interactive Modeling, another month looking at how her students are progressing with sharing at Morning Meeting, and still another month working harder to incorporate academics into her Morning Meetings. She is excited to begin another stage of the assessment process and decides to evaluate and examine her practice in Section IV: Guided Discovery. She begins her learning cycle anew.

FOR SPECIAL AREA TEACHERS

Special area teachers who have had *Responsive Classroom* training may wish to assess their *Responsive Classroom* practice by using the assessment tool. However, they may have to adapt the instrument to their circumstances. For instance, most special area teachers do not have a long or structured arrival time or time for a complete Morning Meeting, and so will need to be selective in choosing the parts of the assessment tool that apply to their practice. Nonetheless, the assessment tool can lead special area teachers to reflect deeply on many aspects of their *Responsive Classroom* practice, such as Interactive Modeling, classroom management, teacher language, logical consequences, and classroom organization.

 ### Generating Ideas and Goals: Establishing Purposes and Choosing Appropriate Sections of the Assessment Tool

Special area teachers should decide which components of the assessment apply to their practice. They might decide that some, like arrival time, do not apply at all. For others, like Morning Meeting, they may want to use some parts of the section that apply to what they do to start their classes.

Once these teachers have identified which parts of the tool apply, some may decide to assess all of those components at one time to obtain a complete view of their *Responsive Classroom* practice. They could assess each of the items that apply to their practice over the course of a day or several days.

Other special area teachers might prefer to assess themselves on only one or two components at a time. For example, some might choose to begin with what they think are areas of relative strength and then use the assessment tool to identify whether their perceptions are accurate and look for changes or adjustments to refine those areas of strength even further before slowly looking at other areas of implementation. Others might want to begin with a problem area and use the assessment tool to help them target why that area seems troublesome and how to improve it.

After selecting their purposes and appropriate sections, special area teachers need to decide what, if anything, they will do to prepare for using the assessment tool:

- Some special area teachers may prefer to have their first use of the assessment tool occur "cold" with no preparation or reflection. They will simply identify the area of practice on which they want to focus and begin to rate themselves on the various items within this area. They might feel that such an initial assessment would give the most accurate view of their practice.

- Other special area teachers may be interested in some pre-assessment reflection exercises (provided at the beginning of each section of the tool). These exercises will help them think about what they already know about a particular topic, identify questions that they may have, and set the stage to reflect more deeply later on about what they discover through the assessment process.

- Some special area teachers may prefer to review relevant resources (see pages 38–63) before they assess themselves on their implementation. This could make the assessment process richer for them.

Actively Exploring, Experimenting, and Solving Problems:
Administering the Assessment Tool

To use the instrument itself, teachers should follow these steps:

1 Read each item carefully to be sure you understand which aspect of your practice you are assessing. If you are observing another teacher, be sure to read each item beforehand to make sure you understand exactly what you will be looking for as you observe.

2 For each item, circle the rating (the number 1, 3, or 5) that best describes the item being observed. If you cannot decide between two ratings, mark the lower number. The mere fact of uncertainty indicates that this item may be one that needs further effort. Do not be concerned if the ratings are not all 5's for any particular section or for the whole assessment process. The assessment tool is designed to present a range of implementation with 5 often representing the ideal. Most teachers, even those who have been using *Responsive Classroom* practices well for long periods of time, will have areas in which they find room for improvement.

3 After completing an entire section, calculate the average score for the section:

- Add up the total points for that section.

- Divide that number by the number of items in that section. Any item that is not answered (for instance, because this practice is not used) should be scored as a zero and the zero should be calculated into the average score. There are a few items that can be scored as nonapplicable (n/a). Do not use these items to calculate the average score.

4 Look at the average scores and determine what they mean for you:

An average of …	Indicates that …
4.0 or above	Your implementation is strong
3.0–3.9	You are making good progress
Less than 3.0	You need to strengthen your implementation

5 If you are working on completing all eight sections, when you have done so, complete the final summary page included with the assessment tool. This will give you an overall picture of your current *Responsive Classroom* practice.

Reflecting Upon Experiences: Using the Results to Form an Action Plan

Getting a rating with the assessment tool is just one step in the learning process. Some teachers may want to complete the summary reflection questions included at the end of each section before moving on to another section. These questions are designed to help special area teachers set some goals for further learning and refinement related to the component or practice they are assessing. They may also want to reflect more generally and form an action plan as to what the next steps in the learning process will be. They may want to formulate a plan of improvement using some of the ideas and resources listed on pages 38–63 of this guide.

EXAMPLE:
How Mr. Merrick used the assessment tool as a special area teacher

Mr. Merrick teaches music to students in kindergarten through sixth grade. He attended the Responsive Classroom Course along with all the teachers in his school. He enjoyed the training and has tried to put much of what he learned into his teaching practice, but he still finds that he struggles considerably with managing students' behavior. He is interested in using the assessment tool to help him identify why he and his classes might be experiencing such difficulties.

Generating Ideas and Goals: Establishing Purposes and Choosing Appropriate Sections of the Assessment Tool

Mr. Merrick decides to begin by focusing on the practice of Interactive Modeling because he has been trying to implement this practice in all of his classes. He decides to do some pre-evaluation reflection and reading.

Mr. Merrick's Pre-Assessment Reflection

1. Reflect on what you currently know about the area of practice you are planning to assess.

—You should use modeling to tell students about behaviors you want them to demonstrate.

—You should have students demonstrate and practice the behaviors.

—You should ask "What do you notice?" during a modeling lesson so that you can be sure students are noticing behaviors you want them to notice.

2. Thoroughly read through this section of the assessment. Note ideas that confirm your best understanding of this practice and ideas that raise questions for you. Think about what the most important goals of this practice are.

—I'm not sure I have been following all the steps correctly, but I wonder if that matters? I think I might want another teacher who has had Responsive Classroom training to help me with this issue.

—I think the most important goal of Interactive Modeling is for teachers to be clear about what they expect so that students will know what to do. But I want to look at this practice in more depth.

3. If you have many questions or potential misunderstandings about this practice, you may want to refer to some of the resources listed in the guide (pp. 38–63) before you assess yourself with the assessment tool.

—I looked back at the Responsive Classroom Course Resource Book for the steps of Interactive Modeling. I'm still not sure if I'm following all of the steps correctly. I don't think that I always say clearly what I'm modeling and why it's important. I'm not really sure how to do this. It's sometimes easier for me to just point out what children are doing wrong and tell them what they need to do.

4. Complete the section assessment.

After doing this reflection and reading, he is beginning to think that perhaps there are problems with his implementation of Interactive Modeling. He realizes that there may be aspects of the practice that he does not fully incorporate into his use of it.

On the basis of his concerns, Mr. Merrick decides that it may be better to have a colleague administer the assessment tool so that he will have another set of eyes focusing on this practice and can discuss it with someone who has more experience with *Responsive Classroom* practices. He turns to a classroom teacher, Mrs. Kennedy, who has been fully trained in *Responsive Classroom* and is known throughout the school for having a great deal of success using *Responsive Classroom* practices.

Mr. Merrick and Mrs. Kennedy decide that because Interactive Modeling lessons are so quick, it would be helpful for her to observe two lessons and base her ratings on both of those in combination. In his first lesson, Mr. Merrick uses Interactive Modeling to show children how to move from the risers on which they practice singing and instrument playing, to their seats where they receive more direct instruction. He has found such transitions difficult.

He uses the second lesson to focus on care of instruments. He has been frustrated that many students are being careless with some of the musical instruments he lets them use in class and are failing to put them away properly. He decides to do an Interactive Modeling lesson on the care and use of the recorders with the third grade students, who are learning to play that instrument.

 Actively Exploring, Experimenting, and Solving Problems: Administering the Assessment Tool

On the basis of the two chosen lessons, Mrs. Kennedy completes the assessment tool for Mr. Merrick. Her individual scores are reflected as follows.

Mr. Merrick's Interactive Modeling assessment completed by his colleague, Mrs. Kennedy

IM 1 Introducing the Modeling I…	(1)	3	5
	… do not name the key behavior positively. *For example, I might say, "We need to line up without fighting or taking a long time."*	… do name the key behavior positively but not briefly or concretely. *For example, I might say, "We need to line up respectfully and responsibly because that helps everyone have a good day and it follows our school rules."*	… do name the key behavior positively, concretely, and briefly. *For example, I might say, "We need to line up in a way that is quick, friendly, and safe."*

IM 2	**(1)**	**3**	**5**
Use of Modeling When teaching a new behavior or reviewing expectations for key behaviors, I . . .	. . . *often* describe the behavior; *I do not model* or have students model it.	. . . *sometimes* model or have a student model the behavior and *sometimes* describe it.	. . . *usually* model or have a student model the behavior.
IM 3	**1**	**(3)**	**5**
Student Modeling When I teach a new behavior or review expectations for key behaviors . . .	. . . *seldom or never* after a behavior is first modeled do I or students model the behavior again.	. . . *sometimes* after a behavior is first modeled, one or more students also model the desired behavior.	. . . *every or almost every* time after a behavior is first modeled, one or more students also model the desired behavior.
IM 4	**1**	**(3)**	**5**
Student Response to Modeling After I or the students model a behavior . . .	. . . we *do not* identify key components, such as when shaking hands, use eye contact, firm grip, etc.	. . . I *tell students* key components, such as when shaking hands, use eye contact, firm grip, etc.	. . . I *ask students* to identify key components, such as when shaking hands, use eye contact, firm grip, etc.
IM 5	**1**	**3**	**(5)**
Student Practice Once students have observed demonstrations of the desired behavior . . .	. . . students *do not* practice the desired behavior while I observe and give feedback.	. . . *many* students practice the desired behavior while I observe and give feedback.	. . . *all or almost all* students practice the desired behavior while I observe and give feedback.

Interactive Modeling   Total number of points* = __13__ divided by 5 items = __2.6__ (average)

Note: Items that you do not rate should be assigned a point value of zero.

Mr. Merrick's overall score for Interactive Modeling is 2.6, indicating that Mr. Merrick was correct in thinking that he needed to strengthen his implementation of Interactive Modeling.

Reflecting Upon Experiences: Using the Results to Form an Action Plan

At first, Mr. Merrick is discouraged by the assessment number, but he completes the post-assessment reflection questions:

Mr. Merrick's Post-Assessment Reflection

Average score __2·6__   **Strength area:**   **Good progress:**   **Area to be improved:**

(average: 4.0 or more)   (average: 3.0–3.9)   (average: less than 3.0)

1. What is an area of particular strength with this practice? What has contributed to your success?

At first, I was not sure I had any strengths, but if I had to identify some I would say that:

—I am pretty clear in my own mind about what I expect from students.

—I try to involve students in the Interactive Modeling process but maybe not enough?

2. What would you identify as areas for improvement?

—I need to use more positive language to begin an Interactive Modeling lesson. I realize that I have been telling them why certain things are problems and not explaining why it is important to do things the way I am showing them.

—I have been telling students what to do rather than demonstrating what to do.

—I don't give students a real chance to answer "What did you notice?" after a student volunteer models the behavior. I am so focused on what I want them to notice that I jump in to tell them myself.

3. Prioritize these areas for improvement in order of most importance to you.

—I think I can work on all three areas at the same time by trying some new Interactive Modeling lessons and being more conscious about following all the steps for those.

4. For your first area of priority, create a self-improvement plan (use notes page if needed). See suggestions in the strategies and resources section for specific ideas about ways to work on one or more of the components of this practice.

—I like the idea in the strategies section of writing out and using a script. I'm going to try that. I also think I'll videotape a lesson. I may also write out some specific teacher language to use.

5. Continue this process with other priority areas.

6. When will you assess this practice again?

—I want to try a few lessons with the scripts and videotaping. Then, I think I will reassess my progress.

Mr. Merrick's self-reflections and his talks with Mrs. Kennedy help him identify some strengths with regard to Interactive Modeling. He also begins to realize that with just some small changes, he could considerably improve his practice.

In terms of strengths, Mr. Merrick realizes that:

■ He generally is clear in his own mind about what he expects from students. Mrs. Kennedy points out that the problem with some teachers is that they are not sure how they want children to perform certain tasks and accordingly cannot explain their expectations to students. Because he has the needed clarity, Mr. Merrick will be able, with some adjustments to his practice, to make his guidelines and expectations very clear for his students.

■ He understands that one key part of Interactive Modeling is involving students in the process. Although he has not included them as completely as he could, he recognizes this key difference between traditional modeling and Interactive Modeling.

Together, Mrs. Kennedy and Mr. Merrick then assess some areas in which he needs to improve:

■ Mr. Merrick has been introducing his Interactive Modeling lessons in a negative way by telling students what he does not want to see. He is beginning to wonder whether using more positive language will help these lessons meet with greater success.

■ He also realizes that he has been telling students what to do rather than demonstrating what to do. Mrs. Kennedy and he discuss how this practice is problematic for several reasons. It does not give students the power of the visual. Students also tend to tune out what they view as "teacher talk" and may not be focusing as much as they would if he demonstrated the behavior and invited them to notice what he did. He realizes that involving students more completely may be especially powerful for students who struggle with behavior, and in many ways, these are the students he is trying hardest to reach. Another problem is that when he talks through behaviors and then has a student volunteer model them, the student has often missed some key aspect of the behavior and either models it incorrectly or has to re-model it under further guidance from Mr. Merrick.

- Mr. Merrick often appropriately asks the class, "What did you notice?" after a student volunteer models the behavior. But he frequently jumps in with his own specific information rather than waiting to see what the class has to say or whether students can identify the key aspects of the behavior. He realizes that he is not involving students as much as he could, again encouraging them to tune out what he has to say.

Mr. Merrick decides to begin working on Interactive Modeling by reteaching the lesson on taking care of recorders.

- He decides to plan the lesson with Mrs. Kennedy and together they write out a "script" for the lesson:

Outline and script for reteaching the care of recorders

- Say what you will model and why.

   "One of your classroom's traveling rules is that you will take care of materials. Today we are going to discuss how to take care of the recorders so that they last all year and sound as beautiful as possible."

- The teacher demonstrates the positive behavior.

   "Watch as I show you how to care for the recorder. See what I do."

   I want to be sure to

   1. slowly remove the recorder from the bag;
   2. hold it upright while playing it;
   3. hold it in my lap while at rest;
   4. place it carefully back in its bag; and
   5. walk over and put the recorder in the communal basket.

- Ask students what they noticed.

"What did you notice about how I used the recorder?"

- Ask student volunteers to demonstrate the positive behavior.

  "Who could show us how to handle the recorder in the way that I did?"

- Ask students what they noticed.

  "What did you notice about how _____ used the recorder?"

- Students practice. You observe and coach.

- Give specific feedback.

  "You put the recorders away in their bags. That will keep them safe."

- He also drafts language he can use to give students feedback as students practice the modeled behavior:

Reinforcing language	Reminding language, if needed	Redirecting language, if needed
"Everyone took their recorders out so carefully. I can already tell we are off to a good start with taking care of them." "I see everyone holding their recorders in their laps while I explain what we are going to do next." "All the recorders are back in the basket, and you put them there safely and carefully. What helped us today to take such good care of the recorders?"	"Who remembers how we take the recorder out of the bag?" "Who can remind us where recorders go while I explain the next song?" To child about to pick up a recorder, "_____, remember where recorders go." "Remind us how we put the recorders away."	To child roughly pulling a recorder out of the bag, "Stop. Take the recorder out gently." To child swirling a recorder around in the air as he plays, "_____, show me how to hold the recorder when you play." To child playing with a recorder while teacher is instructing, "_____, recorders are down." To child running over to put a recorder in the basket, "_____, walk."

- Mr. Merrick also plans to have the script next to him as he teaches it. He hopes to stick firmly to some of the language he and Mrs. Kennedy wrote.

- He decides to have the lesson videotaped so that he and Mrs. Kennedy can watch it together.

After the lesson is taught, Mrs. Kennedy and Mr. Merrick meet, watch the videotape, and discuss their observations and impressions. They both agree that the newly designed lesson was more effective and better taught. Mr. Merrick believes that demonstrating the behavior, rather than talking about it, was much more powerful for his students. He also notices that by specifically telling students to model the behavior *in the same way that he demonstrated it*, he did not have to critique the way they modeled or have them re-model. Further, Mr. Merrick finds that by preparing some teacher language ahead of time, he was able to be more positive and direct with his language.

In watching the video, Mr. Merrick notices that he still jumped in rather quickly if, once he asked students what they noticed, they did not come up with answers or the aspects of the behavior he had wanted right away. He decides to plan a different modeling lesson and repeat the process but focus especially on providing wait time for students and using questioning to guide students if they do not identify certain aspects of behavior, rather than telling them. He also decides to keep his focus on Interactive Modeling for awhile and have Mrs. Kennedy come back and reassess in a few months. After that, he plans for his next step to be using the classroom management and teacher language section of the assessment tool.

FOR TEAMS OF TEACHERS

A team of teachers can identify one or more aspects of *Responsive Classroom* practice on which they want to focus jointly, and they can use the assessment tool as a way to document their progress toward their identified goal and to spur thinking and reflection around it.

 Generating Ideas and Goals: Establishing Purposes and Choosing Appropriate Sections of the Assessment Tool

The team should choose the focus for which they are using the assessment tool and then decide which parts of the assessment tool will help them analyze their focus topic. For example, a team may choose to examine their Morning Meeting practices. They will then administer only the Morning Meeting section of the self-assessment tool. They will conduct the assessment, look for areas of strength and areas for growth with Morning Meetings, and make a plan of self-improvement. Once the team is comfortable with the progress it has made in one area, it may then choose another target area and begin the learning process anew.

The team needs to decide whether to engage in pre-assessment reflection and reading or just begin the assessment process with no preparation:

■ Some teams may prefer to have their first use of the assessment tool occur "cold" with no preparation or reflection. These teachers will simply identify the area of practice on which they want to focus and begin to rate themselves on the various items within this area. A team may feel that such a stark initial assessment will give the most accurate view of their practice.

■ Other teams may be interested in some pre-assessment reflection exercises (provided at the beginning of each section). These exercises will help teachers think about what they already know about a particular topic, identify questions they may have, and set the stage for deeper reflection about what they discover through the assessment process.

■ Some teams may also want to review relevant resources (a variety of which are included on pages 38–63) to refresh their memory on some of the more salient characteristics and goals of each component or practice to be evaluated before they assess themselves on their implementation. This could make the assessment process richer for some teachers.

 Actively Exploring, Experimenting, and Solving Problems: Administering the Assessment Tool

To use the instrument itself, teachers should follow these steps:

1 Read each item carefully to be sure you understand which aspect of classroom practice you are assessing.

2 For each item, circle the rating (the number 1, 3, or 5) that best describes the item being observed. If you cannot decide between two ratings, mark the lower number. The mere fact of uncertainty indicates that this item may be one that needs further effort. Do not be concerned if the ratings are not all 5's for any particular section or for the whole assessment process. The assessment tool is designed to present a range of implementation with 5 often representing the ideal. Most teachers, even those who have been using *Responsive Classroom* practices well for long periods of time, will have areas in which they find room for improvement.

3 After completing an entire section, calculate the average score for the section by doing the following:

■ Add up the total points for that section.

■ Divide that number by the number of items in that section. Any item that is not answered (for instance, because this practice is not used) should be scored as a zero and the zero should be calculated into the average score. There are a few items that can be scored as nonapplicable (n/a). You should count these items as missing items; do not use them to calculate the average score.

4 Look at the average scores and determine what they mean:

An average of ...	Indicates that ...
4.0 or above	Your implementation is strong
3.0–3.9	You are making good progress
Less than 3.0	You need to strengthen your implementation

 Reflecting Upon Experiences: Using the Results to Form an Action Plan

Once all members of the team have evaluated themselves and/or each other, the team should look for common areas of strength and common areas in which all need to improve. The team should formulate a plan of improvement using some of the ideas and resources contained later in this guide.

E X A M P L E :
How a team of teachers used the assessment tool

The third grade team at P.S. 180 consists of four teachers who plan well together and want to focus on teacher language as an area for team growth this year. All four teachers have attended the Responsive Classroom Course and have read several *Responsive Classroom* books. They are thinking about attending the Responsive Classroom Advanced Course next summer. At their request, their administrator has bought them each a copy of *The Power of Our Words: Teacher Language That Helps Children Learn* as a study book for the year.

Generating Ideas and Goals: Establishing Purposes and
Choosing Appropriate Sections of the Assessment Tool

They decide to use the assessment tool as part of their focus on teacher language. They decide that they will assess their performance with Section 7 of the tool: "Classroom Management and Teacher Language." The third grade teachers have a close working relationship and are comfortable with each other, so they decide that instead of assessing themselves, they will assign one teammate to each teacher and use peer observations. They ask for and receive substitute coverage for these observations.

While looking at the assessment tool, the teachers realize that there may be some items in the "Classroom Management and Teacher Language" section, like those concerning how well a teacher uses time-out or the buddy-teacher procedure, that they may not see in action during the observation and accordingly will not be able to assess. They decide that if there are items that they cannot actually observe, they will leave these items blank and let teachers assess themselves after the observer fills out the rest of the tool.

Actively Exploring, Experimenting, and Solving Problems:
Administering the Assessment Tool

The team completes the assessment tool as planned, using a combination of colleague observation and self-evaluation.

Reflecting Upon Experiences: Using the Results to Form an Action Plan

After completing their observations, the team meets to see if they can see common areas of strength, particularly with regard to teacher language. They decide that they are all:

- Speaking to children with calm, respectful, and matter-of-fact voices

- Using redirecting language by giving brief and nonnegotiable directions in the form of statements

- Using redirecting language to name what they want students to do

- Using redirecting language when they are feeling calm

They also evaluate areas on which they want to focus for growth. These include:

- Using reinforcing language more. The team notices that according to item CM21, they should be using reinforcing language more often than the other types of language. But, during their observations, they notice that they all spent more time on general praise, reminders, and redirections than on reinforcing language. They want to reverse that trend. They also have all struggled with describing specific and concrete behaviors to children and decide that they may need more practice with reinforcing language generally.

- They realize that with reminding language, they have mainly been reminding students by re-explaining to them behavior expectations instead of asking questions or making statements that invite students to remember, reflect on, and demonstrate the desired behavior.

- They are all curious about the item focusing on "voiceovers." All of them realize that they are using voiceovers with their students but want to find out more about what might be wrong with this practice and what they can do as alternatives.

The team decides to begin their process of growth by reading Chapter 5 of *The Power of Our Words*, which focuses on reinforcing language. They meet and discuss the highlights of the chapter. They decide on several ways that they will work to increase and improve their own reinforcing language:

- They first decide to practice using reinforcing language with each other's classes. They hope that it will be easier to use specific and clear language when they do not have responsibilities for teaching content or managing student behavior. They decide to begin by visiting each other during writing workshop time. They decide that they will walk around and give children specific feedback about their writing during this time.

- They also decide to draft some reinforcing language ahead of time that they hope to use with their own classes. They brainstorm situations when they may want to reinforce the whole class's efforts and prepare some language they can use in these situations. They eventually want to be spontaneous with their language, and they think and hope that if they just begin practicing using reinforcing language, even if in fairly rehearsed ways, spontaneity will become easier and more natural for all of them. They draft some language to use with their classes at transition time:

"Everyone took out their writing folders and got to work quickly. Our writing workshop is off to a great start."

"The room is so quiet. That shows me that you are really working hard."

"Many people are referring to our 'What to do when you're finished' chart. Some are rereading their pieces and others have begun illustrating."

"Everyone is listening carefully to our signal. I see pencils down and eyes on me."

"Wow, you moved from your desks to read-aloud fast! You put your papers back in your folders, you put your pencils away, and you came to join me on the carpet. What helped us make such a smooth transition?"

"I saw almost everyone line up quickly with hands at their sides and enough space between all of us. You are ready for recess!"

■ The team also decides, on the basis of their reading of Chapter 5 of *The Power of Our Words*, to be on the lookout for "leading edge" behaviors and to be sure that they are reinforcing students exhibiting such behaviors. They also remind each other to share these observations privately with individual students rather than pointing out these behaviors publicly.

The team decides to take these steps and work on their reinforcing language for about a month. At the end of that month, they decide not to readminister the whole assessment tool. Instead, they decide just to look at CM21, the item on language frequency. They decide that they will go into each other's rooms to observe and will simply tally each time a colleague uses reinforcing, reminding, redirecting, and general praise. They will then look at their ratios and see how they are doing.

Strategies and Resources for Building on Assessment Results

Once teachers have identified an area or areas of *Responsive Classroom* practice in which they want to improve, they may want to develop a plan for how to make those improvements. Some general strategies for developing a self-improvement plan include:

- *Peer coaching or observation.* It can be very beneficial to invite a colleague into your classroom to observe a particular component or practice, to give specific feedback related to areas of strength or growth, and to share ongoing conversations about that feedback and your progress.

- *Videotaping.* Videotaping a particular practice, lesson, or component can often highlight issues you were unaware of. You may even want to administer the assessment tool while watching a videotape segment rather than merely relying on your memory of how you are faring with a given skill or practice.

- *Inviting colleagues to join you in a book study group around an area of* Responsive Classroom *practice.* Once you have identified an area you want to work on, you may want to organize a team to study the area with you. That team could read and study a *Responsive Classroom* book or article or use a professional development tool like the *Morning Meeting* Professional Development Kit.

- *Creating a timeline of your* Responsive Classroom *implementation.* Sometimes merely mapping out the steps you have already taken with regard to *Responsive Classroom* implementation or other initiatives can help you identify future steps for growth. Your timeline should include formal training, books you've read or resources you've used, challenges along the way, classroom or schoolwide practices and when they began, and other experiences that have shaped your successful implementation.

- *Checking out the research that quantifies the effectiveness of* Responsive Classroom *practices in schools (www.responsiveclassroom.org/research).* By looking at the results of this research and noting ways in which these findings are reflected in your own classroom or teaching, you can deepen your understanding of *Responsive Classroom* practices and their power.

In addition, for each of the eight major sections of the assessment tool, we have recommended specific strategies and resources that might help you improve.

SECTION 1: ARRIVAL TIME

Section 1 of the assessment tool is divided into four subsections:

1. Teacher–student interactions

2. Arrival routines

3. Students' behaviors

4. Peer interactions

Teachers should identify an area (or areas) for focused attention and create a plan for improvement. Teachers may want to use some of the suggested strategies or resources included here.

STRATEGIES

- Think about what children see when they enter the classroom. Before the children arrive, walk into the room and look at it through students' eyes. Scan the room and pay attention to visual messages children might receive. Is the classroom an inviting space for children (minimal visual clutter, inviting morning message, tidy and clean space, etc.)? If you see problems or are not sure, you may want to refer to *Classroom Spaces That Work*, Chapter Two: "A Place for Everything and Everything in Its Place."

- Reflect on what you do during arrival time, especially how you support children's positive behaviors and self-management skills during this time.

- Reflect on how well you are using arrival time to get to know your students. One way to do this reflection is to engage in the following exercise Chip Wood discusses in his book *Time to Teach, Time to Learn*. Following this exercise, think about how you might use arrival time to learn more about students and show you're interested in their lives.

Take time to get to know the children

Knowing your children involves more than remembering the things kids tell you about themselves. You need to let the kids know what you know about them. When children know that they are known in the classroom, they feel safer and are better able to use their time in school for learning.

A simple exercise created decades ago by writing expert Donald Graves can help you be more intentional about this process. Try writing down the names of the children in your class from memory, in whatever order they come into your head, and then writing down an interest of the child's or something you know is happening in their life. Then, put a check by the child's name if you are sure you have communicated this to them—i.e., if the child knows you know what they are interested in or what is happening in their life. A check mark means that they know they are known. (From page 242 of Time to Teach, Time to Learn by Chip Wood, Center for Responsive Schools, 1999.)

- Reflect on what the students' responsibilities and routines are during arrival time. Have you made these responsibilities and routines clear and taught them to students? If there are responsibilities and routines you have not made clear, plan Interactive Modeling lessons and discussions to teach those responsibilities and routines.

- Create a list of all of the behaviors that the children have learned that enable them to participate successfully during arrival time. Are there other behaviors that you could add to this list that might help the students meet with even more success? Plan how you might introduce or practice these skills using the Interactive Modeling Planning Sheet (see page 65).

- Reflect on the visual or auditory signals you use during arrival time and how well those are working to gain children's attention. If they are not working well, consider reteaching and practicing these signals using the Interactive Modeling Planning Sheet.

- Invite a colleague in to observe your arrival time routines. Ask for feedback about how well your teacher language and practices support children in independently managing morning routines. Have your colleague use the assessment tool as a guide.

- Audiotape your morning routines. As you listen later, take note of the reinforcing language you use to recognize children's positive behaviors. Analyze your reinforcing language to see if it meets the following criteria:

  → Names concrete and specific behaviors

  → Points out approximations toward mastery

  → May be followed by a question to extend student thinking

  → Applies to all students

  → Emphasizes description over personal approval

  → Reflects important goals and values

- You may also want to analyze your individual interactions with students to see whether you are mainly using this time to give directions or procedural information or whether you are interacting with students in a more personal way.

RESOURCES

All resources are available from
www.responsiveclassroom.org

Arrival Time, *In Our School: Building Community in Elementary Schools*, by Karen Casto and Jennifer R. Audley. Center for Responsive Schools 2008. Pp. 45–48.

The First Six Weeks of School, 2nd ed., by Center for Responsive Schools 2015. (Read chapters related to your grade level.)

The Power of Our Words, 2nd ed., by Paula Denton, EdD. Center for Responsive Schools 2014.

What Every Teacher Needs to Know K–5 series, by Mike Anderson and Margaret Berry Wilson. Center for Responsive Schools 2010–2011.

ADDITIONAL TRAINING/SERVICES AVAILABLE

- Responsive Classroom Course and Responsive Classroom Advanced Course

- Follow-up coaching with a *Responsive Classroom* consultant

SECTION 2: INTERACTIVE MODELING

Section 2 of the assessment tool is divided into five subsections:

1. Introducing the modeling

2. Use of modeling

3. Student modeling

4. Student response to modeling

5. Student practice

Teachers should identify an area (or areas) for focused attention and create a plan for improvement. Teachers may want to use some of the suggested strategies or resources included here.

- Write out scripts for Interactive Modeling lessons. Use those scripts to guide you until you have internalized the process.

- Have a colleague observe you and use either your script or an outline of the steps to document whether you are meeting each step of the process.

- Video an Interactive Modeling lesson. As you review the video, note whether you have:

  → Used brief and clear language to say what you are going to model and why.

  → Given students the opportunity to point out key aspects of the behavior being modeled instead of your talking about those key components.

  → Had one or two students model the behavior after your demonstration.

  → Used reinforcing language to provide specific feedback to students as they practice the behavior. Also, think about whether there are additional behaviors or skills that you could have reinforced.

- Make a list of behaviors for which you have used Interactive Modeling in the past and another list of behaviors for which you have not used this practice but may want to in the future. You may want to confer with a colleague or check some of the resources listed below to see the full range of behaviors for which you can use Interactive Modeling.

- Identify a time of day that is challenging for the students. Create a list of the skills that children need in order to be successful at this time of day. Introduce and practice some of these skills through Interactive Modeling. For example, transition from arrival time to Morning Meeting is challenging for many teachers and students. Some skills that students need to learn and teachers need to teach to make these transitions smooth include:

  → Responding to the signal

  → Knowing what to do if friends around you aren't responding to the signal

  → Knowing how to put morning work away quietly, carefully, and in the right place

  → Coming to the Morning Meeting circle in a quiet and careful way

→ Knowing where and how to sit in the Morning Meeting circle

→ Knowing what to do when arriving late, or when a classmate joins the group late

■ Review the developmental characteristics (from *Yardsticks: Children in the Classroom Ages 4–14*) of the age group that you teach. Think through which of these characteristics might require some focused attention through Interactive Modeling. For example, eight-year-olds tend to be full of energy and do things in a hurry. Which strategies might you need to model to help children take a more careful approach to their work?

RESOURCES

All resources are available
from www.responsiveclassroom.org

Behavior Challenges in the Homestretch. *Responsive Classroom Newsletter.* 2010 (Spring).

Interactive Modeling: A Powerful Technique for Teaching Children, by Margaret Berry Wilson. Center for Responsive Schools 2012.

Teaching Positive Behavior: Bringing the Rules to Life, *Rules in School: Teaching Discipline in the Responsive Classroom*, 2nd ed., by Kathryn Brady, Mary Beth Forton, and Deborah Porter. Center for Responsive Schools 2011. Chapter Two.

Teaching the Skills Needed for Success with Academic Choice, *Learning Through Academic Choice*, by Paula Denton. Center for Responsive Schools 2005. Pp. 15–23.

Yardsticks: Children in the Classroom Ages 4–14, 3rd ed., by Chip Wood. Center for Responsive Schools 2007. (Read chapters that correspond to the ages of the children you teach.)

ADDITIONAL TRAINING/SERVICES AVAILABLE

■ Responsive Classroom Course and Responsive Classroom Advanced Course

■ Follow-up coaching with a *Responsive Classroom* consultant

SECTION 3: MORNING MEETING

Section 3 of the assessment tool is divided into five subsections:

1. General characteristics

2. Greeting

3. Sharing

4. Group activity

5. Morning message

Teachers should identify an area (or areas) for focused attention and create a plan for improvement. They may want to use some of the suggested strategies or resources included here.

STRATEGIES

The four components: greeting, sharing, group activity, morning message

- Keep a running record of Morning Meeting greetings, sharing topics, and/or activities.

  → Reflect on ways in which you scaffold the skills necessary for success with these components, such as building from the simple Different Language Greeting to one with more complex choices over several days.

  → Reflect on whether you are choosing a variety of greetings, sharing topics, and/or activities to reach a wide variety of learning styles and student interests.

  → Think about ways you could work academic content/skills into favorite classroom greetings, sharing topics, and/or activities.

- During the greeting component, pay attention to students' levels of friendly engagement, hospitality, and clear and audible speech. Reflect on which of the following skills are secure with all students: friendly facial gestures, eye contact, greeting a wide range of classmates, firm yet gentle handshakes, positive tone of voice, and knowledge and use of names. Also, observe what the rest of the students do when two students are greeting each other and determine whether these remaining students are focusing on the greeters with respectful attention. If children need work with some of these skills, plan how you might use Interactive Modeling to reteach or practice with them.

- Collect and analyze data for the sharing component. For example, spend a week and take notes about which students share, the topic of their sharing, and the manner of their presentation. Some questions to think about as you analyze the data include:

→ Do students choose a wide range of topics? If not, you may want to brainstorm with students some possible topics and/or reteach the types of news and information appropriate for sharing. Or, you may want to take a few days and do around-the-circle sharing or dialogue sharing with assigned topics.

→ Do sharers provide listeners with important details but not so much as to make sharing overly long?

→ Do sharers speak clearly and with an appropriate volume?

→ Do they respond appropriately to questions or comments?

→ Are there sharing skills that all students seem to be missing that you need to model or re-model?

■ Save your morning messages for a week. Have a colleague look at the messages and give you feedback on these issues:

→ Do your messages generally address one topic?

→ Is the topic chosen one that would engage students and/or motivate them to be more engaged in the learning of the day?

→ Do you vary the topic to include social and academic issues?

→ Do you vary the way students interact with the message (reading, thinking questions, questions requiring a written response, questions requiring a tally or some form of data collection, etc.)? If not, what are some other ways you could have students interact with the message?

→ Are there ways that you have addressed some of the skills on which your class has been working through the use of your message? Are there other ways you could do this?

■ Make a plan for how you will incorporate academic content directly related to your curriculum during Morning Meetings for one week. How might you do this in a fun way that builds community?

General considerations about space, transitions, and length of meetings

■ Time the length of your Morning Meetings for the course of one week. If you are over the recommended twenty to thirty minutes, think about the changes you could make: Do you need smoother transitions, shorter greetings or activities, etc.? If you are generally under fifteen minutes, think about what changes you may need to make to enhance the content of your meetings.

- Take a look at your Morning Meeting space. If there is currently not enough room for a well-spaced circle, think about what you might do to rearrange your space or create more room for all children to sit comfortably and view everyone in the circle.

- Consider whether students are coming to the circle quickly and efficiently. If not, think about ways you could address this issue. Do you need to re-model certain behaviors? Is your class one that would benefit from having more direction about where to sit, such as assigned seats in the circle?

Student engagement in Morning Meeting

- Take a look at the location of your morning message chart. Is there enough room for three to five students to gather around to read and interact with the message? If not, think about how you might create a more welcoming and open space that would support children's engagement and interaction with the message chart.

- Make a list of the things you learn about your students during Morning Meeting. Think about how you might use this information to strengthen your relationships with your students and their relationships with one another. Think about how you might use this information to plan future Morning Meetings.

- Notice positive interactions among your students during Morning Meeting. In what ways are the interactions friendly and respectful of others? Plan how you might increase your use of reinforcing language to recognize children's positive interactions. If you notice that the skills of friendliness and respect are lacking, plan how you might restructure the meeting or expectations to help children meet with more success. For example, if you notice that children are developing a habit of greeting only their best friends, you might plan more structured greetings that allow children to greet a wider variety of peers (Snowball Greeting, Name Card Greeting, Alphabetical Greeting, etc.).

- Think about which developmental characteristics (refer to *Yardsticks*) need to be considered when planning how best to support your student's success with Morning Meeting. For example, nine-year-olds tend to be highly competitive. When planning activities that might trigger competition among students, how might you structure those activities to encourage cooperation and community building?

RESOURCES

All resources are available from
www.responsiveclassroom.org

The Art of Commenting. *Responsive Classroom Newsletter*. 2007 (August).

Doing Language Arts in Morning Meeting, by Jodie Luongo, Joan Riordan, and Kate Umstatter. Center for Responsive Schools 2015.

Doing Math in Morning Meeting, by Andy Dousis and Margaret Berry Wilson. Center for Responsive Schools 2010.

Doing Science in Morning Meeting, by Lara Webb and Margaret Berry Wilson. Center for Responsive Schools 2013.

80 Morning Meeting Ideas for Grades K–2, by Susan Lattanzi Roser. Center for Responsive Schools 2012.

80 Morning Meeting Ideas for Grades 3–6, by Carol Davis. Center for Responsive Schools 2012.

Good Morning, Learners! *Responsive Classroom Newsletter*. 2006 (November).

Group Activities That Reinforce Academic Skills. *Responsive Classroom Newsletter*. 2003 (Winter).

Ideas for Morning Meeting Messages. *Responsive Classroom Newsletter*. 2002 (Fall).

Keeping Morning Meeting Greetings Fresh and Fun: Ideas for Expanding Your Repertoire. *Responsive Classroom Newsletter*. 2000 (Fall).

Lively & Artful Sharings: How Brief Check-ins Can Help Sharers Shine. *Responsive Classroom Newsletter*. 2008 (November).

The Morning Meeting Book, 3rd ed., by Roxann Kriete and Carol Davis. Center for Responsive Schools 2014.

Morning Meeting Greetings. *Responsive Classroom Newsletter*. 2006 (August).

Morning Meeting Messages, K–6, by Rosalea S. Fisher, Eric Henry, and Deborah Porter. Center for Responsive Schools 2006.

Morning Meeting Professional Development Kit. Center for Responsive Schools 2008.

99 Activities and Greetings, by Melissa Correa-Connolly. Center for Responsive Schools 2004.

The Power of Morning Meeting: Like Being at the Breakfast Table. *Responsive Classroom Newsletter.* 2002 (Fall).

Teachers Learn from Visiting Each Other's Morning Meetings. *Responsive Classroom Newsletter.* 2005 (August).

Themed Sharing during Morning Meeting. *Responsive Classroom Newsletter.* 2005 (August).

Yardsticks: Children in the Classroom Ages 4–14, 3rd ed., by Chip Wood. Center for Responsive Schools 2007.

ADDITIONAL TRAINING/SERVICES AVAILABLE

■ Responsive Classroom Course and Responsive Classroom Advanced Course

■ One-day workshop: Morning Meeting and Academics

■ Follow-up coaching with a *Responsive Classroom* consultant

SECTION 4: GUIDED DISCOVERY

Section 4 of the assessment tool is divided into five subsections:

1. General guidelines

2. Introduction

3. Exploration

4. Sharing exploratory work

5. Cleanup

Teachers should identify an area (or areas) for focused attention and create a plan for improvement. They may want to use some of the suggested strategies or resources included here.

STRATEGIES

■ Of the five steps in a Guided Discovery, identify one area in which you would like to develop more facility:

1. Introduction and naming of materials

2. Generating and modeling of students' ideas

3. Exploration

4. Sharing exploratory work

5. Cleanup and care of materials

- Plan ahead for open-ended questions you might use to stimulate children's thinking and to encourage their creative exploration during a Guided Discovery lesson.

- Write out scripts for Guided Discovery lessons. Keep the scripts close as you teach the lessons and use them to guide you.

- With a colleague, write out scripts for Guided Discovery lessons and use those scripts as you teach Guided Discovery lessons. Compare notes with the colleague about how the teaching of the lesson(s) went.

- Have a colleague observe you and use either your script or just a general outline of the steps of Guided Discovery to document whether you are meeting each step of the Guided Discovery process.

- Videotape a Guided Discovery lesson. As you watch the videotape later, note whether:

  → You followed each step of the process.

  → Students were engaged in the lesson and why they were or were not.

  → You used open-ended questions to guide student thinking.

  → You interacted with students individually during the exploration phase of the lesson.

  → You used reinforcing language as you interacted with students.

- Make a list of materials for which you have used Guided Discovery in the past and another list of materials for which you have not used this practice but may want to in the future. You may want to confer with a colleague or look at some of the resources that follow to get more ideas about all the ways in which Guided Discovery can be used.

- Reflect on which developmental considerations are relevant when planning a Guided Discovery lesson for your students. For example, most seven-year-olds have a strong need for routine and closure, and need time to finish their work; they appreciate a "heads-up" that it's time to prepare for transitions. When planning a Guided Discovery, the teacher would use reminders or signals for how much time is remaining for exploration. A teacher should also use Interactive Modeling to review and practice what to do when the signal is given.

RESOURCES

All resources are available from
www.responsiveclassroom.org

Favorite Guided Discoveries. *Responsive Classroom Newsletter.* 2004 (Summer).

The First Six Weeks of School, 2nd ed., by Center for Responsive Schools 2015. (Refer to Sample Schedules.)

Guided Discovery in Action. *Responsive Classroom Newsletter.* 2004 (Summer).

Guided Discovery, *Learning Through Academic Choice*, by Paula Denton, EdD. Center for Responsive Schools 2005. Pp. 31–55.

Open-Ended Questions and Appendix A, *The Power of Our Words*, 2nd ed., by Paula Denton. Center for Responsive Schools 2014. Pp. 47–68 and 149–153.

Teaching Children to Care, by Ruth Sidney Charney. Center for Responsive Schools 2002. Pp. 49–56.

Yardsticks: Children in the Classroom Ages 4–14, 3rd ed., by Chip Wood. Center for Responsive Schools 2007.

ADDITIONAL TRAINING/SERVICES AVAILABLE

- Responsive Classroom Advanced Course

- Follow-up coaching with a *Responsive Classroom* consultant

SECTION 5: ACADEMIC CHOICE

Section 5 of the assessment tool is divided into three subsections:

1. Introduction and planning phase

2. Transition from planning phase to working phase

3. Sharing and reflecting phase

Teachers should identify an area (or areas) for focused attention and create a plan for improvement. They may want to use some of the suggested strategies or resources included here.

- Reflect on whether and how well you have scaffolded to ensure student success with Academic Choice. Some issues to consider include:

  → Have you taught students the basic routines and expectations for independent work time?

  → Have you given your students lots of experiences with making simple choices (for example, where to work, which of two problems to do, or which character to draw)?

  → Have you taught children how to consider and make good choices?

  → Have you taught students how to do a variety of academic activities so that you can offer those activities as meaningful choices during Academic Choice? For instance, you may want to teach them how to make and design a poster, write a friendly letter, etc.

  → Have you introduced the materials you intend to use in future Academic Choice lessons through Guided Discovery lessons?

  → Have you taught students how to collaborate and problem-solve with classmates?

  → Have you begun with simple Academic Choice lessons (limited to one to three choices as to either what to learn or how to learn, but not both) and moved up from there, building upon and reinforcing student success?

If upon reflection, you haven't considered or taught some of the prerequisite skills, make a plan for how you might go back and reteach those skills and plan simpler, more successful Academic Choice lessons. If you need more information about scaffolding for success with Academic Choice, read *Learning Through Academic Choice*, Chapter One: Teaching the Skills Needed for Success with Academic Choice, pages 15–29.

- Have a colleague observe you or videotape yourself for specific aspects of your Academic Choice lesson, such as:

  → Whether your lesson included clear planning, working, and reflecting phases.

  → How engaged students were in the lesson and why they were or were not engaged.

  → How well students managed materials during each phase of the lesson.

  → Whether you used open-ended questions to guide student thinking.

  → Whether you interacted with students individually during the working phase of the lesson.

→ How well students collaborated and solved problems during the working phase of the lesson.

→ Whether you used reinforcing language as you interacted with students.

■ During an Academic Choice lesson, pay attention to your role during the working phase. Reflect upon:

→ How you check in with students and show a genuine interest in their thinking and work.

→ Whether you are able to use information you learn to inform your teaching and meet individual students' needs.

→ Whether you are able to reach all students, not just those who struggle or seek out your assistance.

■ Think about and document how you have had students reflect on their learning. Issues to consider or strategies to try include:

→ Whether you have had students reflect on their work.

→ Whether, when students reflect with others, you have scaffolded the skills students need for success. For instance, consider whether you have taught and practiced these skills with students:

—Briefly summarizing their work

—Responding to an open-ended reflection question

—Demonstrating listening by repeating or paraphrasing what another student shared

—Showing interest through respectful comments

—Asking interested, respectful questions

→ Whether you might use Interactive Modeling and practice to teach and scaffold skills necessary for reflecting with others.

→ Whether you have effectively used open-ended questions to help students reflect on their learning in a variety of ways. For example, "What is one thing you learned from doing this work?" If you are not sure, make a menu of possible open-ended questions you could use. Refer to *Learning Through Academic Choice*, pages 107–110, for reflection ideas..

→ Whether you have clear learning goals stated.

■ In addition to Academic Choice, what other choices do you provide children throughout the day? Are there limited choices that you might offer children that would contribute to a higher level of engagement and positive behaviors? In *Learning Through Academic Choice*, Paula Denton states that "educational researchers—and many teachers—report that students get along better with each other, resolve conflicts more independently, and actually reduce the number of problem behaviors in the classroom when they have regular opportunities to make choices in their learning." Plan how you might increase the number of choices at other times of the day.

RESOURCES

All resources are available from
www.responsiveclassroom.org

Learning Through Academic Choice, by Paula Denton. Center for Responsive Schools 2005.

Many Ways to Learn: Multiple Intelligences Theory Changes Teaching and Learning in a Fourth Grade Classroom. *Responsive Classroom Newsletter*. 2007 (November).

Open-Ended Questions, *The Power of Our Words*, 2nd ed., by Paula Denton, EdD. Center for Responsive Schools 2014. Pp. 47–68.

What Do Insects *Do* All Day? How Academic Choice Can Spark Children's Desire to Learn. *Responsive Classroom Newsletter*. 2006 (January).

ADDITIONAL TRAINING/SERVICES AVAILABLE

■ Responsive Classroom Course and Responsive Classroom Advanced Course

■ Follow-up coaching with a *Responsive Classroom* consultant

SECTION 6: CLASSROOM ORGANIZATION

Section 6 of the assessment tool is divided into seven subsections:

1. Classroom space

2. Furniture arrangement

3. Visibility of students

4. Work spaces

5. Storage of classroom materials

6. Displays and wall decorations: content and presentation

7. Time-out: placement and visibility

Teachers should identify an area (or areas) for focused attention and create a plan for improvement. They may want to use some of the suggested strategies or resources included here.

STRATEGIES

- Ask yourself some focused questions related to the whole-group meeting area:

  → Is there space in your classroom for a whole-group meeting area?

  → Are children able to sit comfortably in a circle where everyone can see and be seen by everyone else?

  → If not, how might you reconfigure your room to make space for this critical area?

  → How often do you use this space and for what purposes?

  → How might you better use this space for a broad range of instructional purposes?

- Map out your classroom on grid or plain paper. Make cut-outs of major parts so that you can move furniture and play around with room arrangement on paper before attempting it with the actual furniture.

- Invite a colleague or group of colleagues to come look at your room with "fresh eyes."

- Take a look at the furniture in your room and ask yourself some pointed questions about it, including:

  → How often do I or the students use this piece of furniture in a given school day? Week? Month?

  → How much room is the furniture taking up, and does the benefit of having that piece of furniture outweigh the amount of space it takes up?

  → Is there a way I can rearrange or reposition particular pieces of furniture to maximize room space and/or get rid of "dead" spaces in my classroom?

- Take a look at the major materials in your room and ask yourself some pointed questions about these, including:

  → How often do I or the students use this material in a given day? Week? Month? Are there some materials in my classroom that I have not used in months or even years?

→ Are there any materials that are in poor working condition or are otherwise uninspiring?

→ Have I clearly separated and marked materials to which I want students to have access and those that are only for my use?

■ Ask yourself about locations in the classroom where children are exhibiting positive behaviors. Think about what elements of your classroom organization might be contributing to positive behaviors and how you might restructure the environment to better support children's success.

■ Ask yourself where in the classroom children are exhibiting challenging behaviors. Think about what elements of your classroom organization might be contributing to these behaviors.

■ Do the birthday cluster exercise (pages 18-20, *Classroom Spaces That Work*). What implications does the developmental "cluster" that you identify hold for your classroom organization? Read through the key growth patterns and classroom setup implications for the grade level you teach (*Classroom Spaces That Work*). How might the developmental needs of your students change as the year progresses, and what will those changes mean for your classroom organization? You may also want to refer to *Yardsticks* for more specific information about developmental characteristics.

■ Reflect on how your classroom organization supports the *Responsive Classroom* principle that the greatest cognitive growth occurs through social interaction.

RESOURCES

All resources are available from
www.responsiveclassroom.org

Classroom Spaces That Work, by Marlynn K. Clayton, with Mary Beth Forton. Center for Responsive Schools 2001.

The Difference Is Amazing: After 17 Years in the Classroom, a First Grade Teacher Makes "Drastic" Changes in the Physical Arrangement of the Classroom. *Responsive Classroom Newsletter.* 2001 (Spring).

Displaying Student Work. *Responsive Classroom Newsletter.* 2002 (Fall).

Getting the Most Value Out of Displays. *Responsive Classroom Newsletter.* 2001 (Fall).

Lessons from the Apartment Classroom. *Responsive Classroom Newsletter.* 2002 (Summer).

Opening Soon. *Responsive Classroom Newsletter.* 2004 (Summer).

Opening the Classroom Library. *Responsive Classroom Newsletter.* 2006 (August).

Q & A: How Classroom Setup Can Enhance Children's Learning. *Responsive Classroom Newsletter.* 2007 (April).

Q & A: Solving the Space Crunch. *Responsive Classroom Newsletter.* 2008 (August).

A Quiet Place for Rough Moments. *Responsive Classroom Newsletter.* 2003 (Spring).

ADDITIONAL TRAINING/SERVICES AVAILABLE

- Responsive Classroom Advanced Course

- Follow-up coaching with a *Responsive Classroom* consultant

SECTION 7: CLASSROOM MANAGEMENT AND TEACHER LANGUAGE

Section 7 of the assessment tool is divided into six subsections:

1. Classroom rules

2. Signals

3. Beginning lessons and activities

4. Transitions

5. Language

6. Logical consequences

Teachers should identify an area (or areas) for focused attention and create a plan for improvement. Teachers may want to use some of the suggested strategies or resources included here.

STRATEGIES

- Watch a *Responsive Classroom* DVD clip with classroom management and teacher language in mind. Notice how the teacher(s) on the DVD did or could have done any of the following:

  → Used Interactive Modeling to show students key behaviors and have them notice important aspects of those behaviors.

  → Organized, planned, or taught the lesson or activity to maximize the potential for student success.

→ Used reinforcing language to give students feedback about how they were behaving or performing academically.

→ Used reminding language proactively to have students think about the challenges of a particular task or activity before undertaking it.

→ Used redirecting language when students were off track.

- Pick one small lesson or a greeting or activity. For each aspect of it, think about things that might go wrong and make a plan for how you will proactively address each of those things.

- Identify times of day or routines that are challenging for students. Plan how you could teach, model, and practice responding to visual and verbal signals and cues and explore other practices that might help children meet with success during these times.

- Plan ahead for reinforcing, reminding, and redirecting language you might use during the teaching of a given greeting, activity, or lesson.

- Observe a colleague's class and practice using reinforcing language to share positive aspects you observed about the behavior or academic accomplishments of that colleague's students.

- Record your language using video or audiotaping. Or, have a colleague record all language you use with regard to children's behavior or performance. Analyze:

  → How many reinforcing, reminding, or redirecting statements you make. Determine the ratio of reinforcing to reminding and redirecting language and whether there is more of the reinforcing language.

  → Whether you used voiceovers during the period of time taped. If you did, think about ways you could begin replacing the voiceovers with a pause, a nod, or, when appropriate, a question that might serve to extend students' thinking.

- Analyze a video or audiotape of your language or a colleague's record of your language regarding children's behavior with an eye toward how you imposed logical consequences. Consider whether you have:

  → Used a respectful tone.

  → Been clear and direct (said what you meant).

  → Been brief.

  → Used words that are firm and do not invite negotiation.

→ Refrained from explaining why the behavior is inappropriate or otherwise trying to justify your consequence.

→ Refrained from lecturing while delivering the consequence.

■ On your own, or with the colleague's help, also analyze the consequences themselves for whether:

→ The consequences you have chosen meet the 3 R's: respectful, relevant, and realistic.

→ You have given consequences for small problems rather than waiting for those to escalate.

→ You missed opportunities to use consequences.

→ You have used consequences with many children or just a few.

■ Using the following grid or some other format, keep a record for a day or week of logical consequences you use. Review the record and reflect upon:

→ Which of the three types of consequences you used and how often you used each one.

→ Whether you are using consequences for small misbehaviors rather than waiting for those to escalate to bigger issues.

Type of consequence used	Tally if used for small problem	Tally if used for big issue	Name each student who received consequence Add tallies for each time used with that student	Tally if the consequence you chose and used met the 3 R's (respectful, relevant, realistic)
Time-out				
You break it, you fix it				
Loss of privilege				

→ How many different students faced consequences. Are the same few students the main ones receiving consequences, or are you using consequences with many students?

→ Whether the consequences you chose were consistently respectful, relevant, and realistic. If not, how could you choose consequences that have these characteristics?

■ Read the newsletter article "Refusing to Go to Time-Out." Identify proactive structures and practices that you will implement to strengthen the effective use of time-out in your classroom. If children are resisting going to time-out, how might you revisit, reteach, and practice this important routine or modify the language you use to support children's successful engagement with this practice? What is your back-up plan if children refuse to go to time-out? Share your plans with a colleague.

RESOURCES

All resources are available from
www.responsiveclassroom.org

Buddy Teachers. *Responsive Classroom Newsletter.* 2005 (Winter).

A Fresh Start Leads to Learning. *Responsive Classroom Newsletter.* 2008 (November).

Hopes, Goals, and Classroom Rules. *Responsive Classroom Newsletter.* 2006 (January).

Open-Ended Questions: Stretching Children's Academic and Social Learning. *Responsive Classroom Newsletter.* 2007 (February).

Positive Time-Out. *Responsive Classroom Newsletter.* 2004 (Winter).

Power in Speech. *Responsive Classroom Newsletter.* 2005 (Winter).

The Power of Our Words, 2nd ed., by Paula Denton, EdD. Center for Responsive Schools 2014.

Punishment vs. Logical Consequences. *Responsive Classroom Newsletter.* 1998 (Summer).

Refusing to Go to Time-Out. *Responsive Classroom Newsletter.* 2002 (Spring).

Revisiting Classroom Rules. *Responsive Classroom Newsletter.* 2005 (Winter).

Rules in School: Teaching Discipline in the Responsive Classroom, 2nd ed., by Kathryn Brady, Mary Beth Forton, and Deborah Porter. Center for Responsive Schools 2011.

Teacher Language Professional Development Kit. Center for Responsive Schools 2010.

Teaching Children to Care, by Ruth Sidney Charney. Center for Responsive Schools 2002.

Teaching Discipline in the Classroom Professional Development Kit. Center for Responsive Schools 2011.

Teasing, Tattling, Defiance and More: Positive Approaches to 10 Common Classroom Behaviors, by Margaret Berry Wilson. Center for Responsive Schools 2013.

What Did You Say? Using Nonverbal Communication to Improve Teacher Effectiveness. *Responsive Classroom Newsletter*. 2003 (Fall).

What Teaching Matthew Taught Me. *Responsive Classroom Newsletter*. 2007 (April).

ADDITIONAL TRAINING/SERVICES AVAILABLE

- Responsive Classroom Course and Responsive Classroom Advanced Course

- One-day workshop: Responding to Misbehavior

- Follow-up coaching with a *Responsive Classroom* consultant

SECTION 8: WORKING WITH FAMILIES

Section 8 of the assessment tool is divided into five subsections:

1. Welcoming and valuing families

2. Families as active participants

3. Communicating with families

4. Sharing information and children's work

5. Problem-solving with families

Teachers should identify an area (or areas) for focused attention and create a plan for improvement. Teachers may want to use some of the suggested strategies or resources included here.

STRATEGIES

- Think about the ways in which you engage parents in articulating and sharing their hopes and dreams for their children. Speak with your colleagues about strategies that they have used to invite parent input and sharing. Are there ideas that you would like to try? Develop a plan to encourage more parental input and sharing around academic and social hopes and dreams.

- Think about how you go about welcoming and including parents in the classroom and school community. Think through an established practice (Open House, Parents' Night, Parent Conferences, Morning Meeting, Family Night, etc.). How have you communicated the goals and expectations for these visits? How might you better structure these experiences so that parent-child, parent-teacher, and/or parent-parent relationships are strengthened?

- Reflect on whether and in what ways you help families understand your approach to rules and logical consequences. How have you communicated your rule-establishing process and the *Responsive Classroom* approach to discipline? Plan how you will continue this communication throughout the school year.

- Keep a portfolio of communication with families. Include classroom newsletters, parent surveys, parent meetings, phone calls, conference notes, etc. Review your portfolio after the first six weeks of school. What have you learned about your students and their families and how do you use this information?

- Keep track of the number of communications you have with the families of each student in your classroom. How many of these communications involve sharing positive news? Plan how you might increase the number of positive communications.

- Reflect on the practices that have helped you learn about the cultures of the families of your students. Plan how you might integrate some of these cultural elements into your classroom. (For example, you might invite parents to visit the classroom to share about their culture or help create classroom resources and curricular connections, etc.)

- Create a plan for communicating collaboratively with parents around a student's academic or behavioral challenges. Generate a list of open-ended questions that might help you to further understand a problem and invite more input from the parents. Before the conference, pay attention to skills and behaviors the child is able to use successfully, so that you are able to describe both positive and challenging behaviors.

RESOURCES

All resources are available from
www.responsiveclassroom.org

Bridging Home and School. *Responsive Classroom Newsletter.* 2004 (Summer).

Families' Hopes and Dreams. *Responsive Classroom Newsletter.* 2003 (Fall).

In Our School, by Karen Casto and Jennifer R. Audley. Center for Responsive Schools 2008.

Investing in Parents during the First Six Weeks. *Responsive Classroom Newsletter.* 2005 (August).

Keeping Connected. *Responsive Classroom Newsletter.* 2004 (Winter).

Like Talking With a Teammate: Informality Enhances Parent Meetings. *Responsive Classroom Newsletter.* 2007 (February).

Morning Meeting Begins at 7:15 p.m.! *Responsive Classroom Newsletter.* 2003 (Summer).

Parents and Teachers Working Together, by Carol Davis and Alice Yang. Center for Responsive Schools 2005.

Rules in School: Teaching Discipline in the Responsive Classroom, 2nd ed., by Kathryn Brady, Mary Beth Forton, and Deborah Porter. Center for Responsive Schools 2011.

Sharing the *Responsive Classroom* Approach With Parents. *Responsive Classroom Newsletter.* 2007 (February).

Teaching Children to Care, by Ruth Sidney Charney. Center for Responsive Schools 2002.

Three-Way Conferences. *Responsive Classroom Newsletter.* 2005 (Spring).

Welcoming All Families. *Responsive Classroom Newsletter.* 2003 (Summer).

Welcoming Families of Different Cultures. *Responsive Classroom Newsletter.* 2006 (April).

When Parents Visit the Classroom, *Off to a Good Start: Launching the School Year,* by Marlynn Clayton. Center for Responsive Schools 1997. Pp. 57–62.

Wonderful Wednesdays. *Responsive Classroom Newsletter.* 2004 (Fall).

Working With Families. *Responsive Classroom Newsletter.* 2001 (Winter).

N O T E S

NOTES

Interactive Modeling Planning Sheet

1. Say what you will model and why. (One or two sentences.)

2. Demonstrate the behavior. (What will you do?)

3. Ask students what they noticed about the behavior demonstrated. (What questions will you ask? What do you want to be sure children understand?)

4. Ask student volunteers to demonstrate the same behavior. (How will you set this up? What will you say?)

5. Repeat step 3. (What questions will you ask? What behavior do you want to highlight?)

6. Students practice. You observe and coach. (How will you prepare the students to use this behavior during the school day? How will they know your expectations?)

7. Give specific feedback.

Section 1. Arrival Time

PRE-ASSESSMENT REFLECTION

I. Reflect on what you currently know about the area of practice you are planning to assess.

II. Thoroughly read through this section of the assessment tool. Note ideas that confirm your best understanding of this practice and ideas that raise questions for you. Think about what the most important goals of this practice are.

III. If you have many questions or potential misunderstandings about this practice, you may want to refer to some of the resources listed in the guide before you assess yourself with the assessment tool.

IV. Complete the section assessment.

Section 1: Arrival Time ☀ Date assessed _____

	1	**3**	**5**
AT 1 **Teacher-Student Interaction** As students arrive in my classroom, I …	… am busy with preparations for the day or other tasks, and I usually interact individually with only a *few* students as they enter the classroom.	… welcome and interact individually with *many* students as they enter the classroom.	… welcome and interact individually with *all or almost all* students as they enter the classroom, and the majority of individual interactions are personal rather than procedural (that is, the majority of interactions show that I know students on a personal level and are not centered on students going about the morning routine).
AT 2 **Arrival Routines** The routines I want students to follow as they arrive in our classroom …	… vary from day to day and/or I need to describe or remind students of directions on many mornings.	… are consistent most days and I have clearly explained (and perhaps posted) these arrival routines.	… are consistent most days and I have taught them to the students by using Interactive Modeling, practice, and reinforcing language.

	1	**3**	**5**
AT 3 **Students' Behavior at Arrival Time** At arrival time ...	... *most* students are noisy, disorganized, or preoccupied with friendship issues.	... *many or most* students demonstrate calm behavior, use soft or medium voices, and know their morning tasks.	... *all or almost all* students demonstrate calm behavior, use soft or medium voices, and know their morning tasks.
AT 4 **Students' Behavior at Arrival Time** At arrival time ...	... *few* students respond quickly to redirection, check-in, or logical consequences whenever expectations for calm behavior, soft or medium voices, and completion of morning tasks are not met.	... *many or most* students respond quickly to redirection, check-in, or logical consequences whenever expectations for calm behavior, soft or medium voices, and completion of morning tasks are not met.	... *all or almost all* students respond quickly to redirection, check-in, or logical consequences whenever expectations for calm behavior, soft or medium voices, and completion of morning tasks are not met.
AT 5 **Peer Interactions at Arrival Time** At arrival time ...	... *few* students respectfully interact with their classmates and exhibit community-oriented behavior *(that is, friendly faces and language, sharing ideas, helping each other, boys and girls working with one another, students of different races working with one another).*	... *many or most* students respectfully interact with their classmates *(that is, friendly faces and language, sharing ideas, helping each other, boys and girls working with one another, students of different races working with one another).*	... *all or almost all* students respectfully interact with their classmates *(that is, friendly faces and language, sharing ideas, helping each other, boys and girls working with one another, students of different races working with one another).*

Arrival Time   Total number of points* = _____ divided by 5 items = _____ (average)

Note: Items that you do not rate should be assigned a point value of zero.

POST-ASSESSMENT REFLECTION

Average score _____ **Strength area:** **Good progress:** **Area to be improved:**

(average: 4.0 or more) (average: 3.0–3.9) (average: less than 3.0)

1. What is an area of particular strength with this practice? What has contributed to your success?

2. What would you identify as areas for improvement?

3. Prioritize these areas for improvement in order of most importance to you.

4. For your first area of priority, create a self-improvement plan (use notes page if needed).
   See suggestions in the strategies and resources section for specific ideas about ways to work
   on one or more of the components of this practice.

5. Continue this process with other priority areas.

6. When will you assess this practice again?

NOTES

Section 2. Interactive Modeling

PRE-ASSESSMENT REFLECTION

I. Reflect on what you currently know about the area of practice you are planning to assess.

II. Thoroughly read through this section of the assessment tool. Note ideas that confirm your best understanding of this practice and ideas that raise questions for you. Think about what the most important goals of this practice are.

III. If you have many questions or potential misunderstandings about this practice, you may want to refer to some of the resources listed in the guide before you assess yourself with the assessment tool.

IV. Complete the section assessment.

Section 2. Interactive Modeling ✳ Date assessed _____

	1	3	5
IM 1 **Introducing the Modeling** I ...	... do not name the key behavior positively. *For example, I might say, "We need to line up without fighting or taking a long time."*	... do name the key behavior positively but not briefly or concretely. *For example, I might say, "We need to line up respectfully and responsibly because that helps everyone have a good day and it follows our school rules."*	... do name the key behavior positively, concretely, and briefly. *For example, I might say, "We need to line up in a way that is quick, friendly, and safe."*
	1	**3**	**5**
IM 2 **Use of Modeling** When teaching a new behavior or reviewing expectations for key behaviors, I ...	... *often* describe the behavior; *I do not model* or have students model it.	... *sometimes* model or have a student model the behavior and *sometimes* describe it.	... *usually* model or have a student model the behavior.

IM 3 **Student Modeling** When I teach a new behavior or review expectations for key behaviors …	**1** … *seldom or never* after a behavior is first modeled do I or students model the behavior again.	**3** … *sometimes* after a behavior is first modeled, one or more students also model the desired behavior.	**5** … *every or almost every* time after a behavior is first modeled, one or more students also model the desired behavior.
IM 4 **Student Response to Modeling** After I or the students model a behavior …	**1** … we *do not* identify key components, such as when shaking hands, use eye contact, firm grip, etc.	**3** … I *tell students* key components, such as when shaking hands, use eye contact, firm grip, etc.	**5** … I *ask students* to identify key components, such as when shaking hands, use eye contact, firm grip, etc.
IM 5 **Student Practice** Once students have observed demonstrations of the desired behavior …	**1** … students *do not* practice the desired behavior while I observe and give feedback.	**3** … *many* students practice the desired behavior while I observe and give feedback.	**5** … *all or almost all* students practice the desired behavior while I observe and give feedback.

Interactive Modeling   Total number of points* = _____ divided by 5 items = _____ (average)

Note: Items that you do not rate should be assigned a point value of zero.

Average score _____   **Strength area:**   **Good progress:**   **Area to be improved:**

                                (average: 4.0 or more)   *(average: 3.0–3.9)*   *(average: less than 3.0)*

1. What is an area of particular strength with this practice? What has contributed to your success?

2. What would you identify as areas for improvement?

3. Prioritize these areas for improvement in order of most importance to you.

4. For your first area of priority, create a self-improvement plan (use notes page if needed). See suggestions in the strategies and resources section for specific ideas about ways to work on one or more of the components of this practice.

5. Continue this process with other priority areas.

6. When will you assess this practice again?

NOTES

Section 3. Morning Meeting

PRE-ASSESSMENT REFLECTION

I.   Reflect on what you currently know about the area of practice you are planning to assess.

II. Thoroughly read through this section of the assessment tool. Note ideas that confirm your best understanding of this practice and ideas that raise questions for you. Think about what the most important goals of this practice are.

III. If you have many questions or potential misunderstandings about this practice, you may want to refer to some of the resources listed in the guide before you assess yourself with the assessment tool.

IV. Complete the section assessment.

Section 3. Morning Meeting ✳ Date assessed _____

G E N E R A L

	1	**3**	**5**
MM 1 **Space** In our Morning Meetings …	… *few* students have room to sit comfortably in a circle/oval and view everyone and everything.	… *most* students have room to sit comfortably in a circle/oval and view everyone and everything.	… *all* students have room to sit comfortably in a circle/oval and view everyone and everything.
MM 2 **Transition to Meeting** When it's time for Morning Meeting to begin …	… *few* students come quickly, quietly, and empty-handed on most days.	… *many* students come quickly, quietly, and empty-handed on most days.	… *most* students come quickly, quietly, and empty-handed on most days.
MM 3 **Processes** During many Morning Meetings, students respond to my designation of our greeting, sharing, and/or group activity with …	… an *extended* amount of negotiation or complaining.	… a *moderate* amount of negotiation or complaining.	… *little or no* negotiation or complaining.

	1	**3**	**5**
MM 4 **Academic Content of the Four Components** (Greeting, Sharing, Group Activity, Morning Message) In our Morning Meetings . . .	. . . usually *no* components incorporate academic content directly related to our curriculum or student needs.	. . . usually *one* component incorporates academic content directly related to our curriculum or student needs.	. . . usually *two or more* components incorporate academic content directly related to our curriculum or student needs in a fun way that builds community.
MM 5 **Length** Morning Meetings in our class . . .	. . . *frequently* last less than twenty minutes or more than thirty minutes.	. . . *sometimes* last approximately twenty to thirty minutes.	. . . *usually* last approximately twenty to thirty minutes.
MM 6 **Order** Morning Meetings in our class . . .	. . . *usually do not* follow the order of (1) greeting, (2) sharing, (3) group activity, and (4) morning message.	. . . *sometimes do* follow the order of (1) greeting, (2) sharing, (3) group activity, and (4) morning message.	. . . *usually do* follow the order of (1) greeting, (2) sharing, (3) group activity, and (4) morning message.
MM 7 **Student Participation** During our Morning Meetings . . .	. . . *many* students leave for breaks, errands, or previously scheduled tasks or sessions.	. . . *most* students remain (that is, only one or two students leave the meeting for breaks, errands, or previously scheduled sessions).	. . . *all* students usually remain (that is, students rarely miss Morning Meeting for any reason).

MM 8 **Teaching Greetings** In general, before the class does a greeting, I ...	**1** ... *do not* usually use Interactive Modeling to teach or remind children about expectations for behavior during the greeting (Interactive Modeling consists of the teacher and one or more students demonstrating expected behavior, students identifying key behaviors, and all students practicing).	**3** ... *sometimes* use Interactive Modeling to teach and review appropriate behavior during the greeting or *regularly* use portions of Interactive Modeling (Interactive Modeling consists of the teacher and one or more students demonstrating expected behavior, students identifying key behaviors, and all students practicing).	**5** ... *regularly* use Interactive Modeling to teach and review appropriate behavior during the greeting (Interactive Modeling consists of the teacher and one or more students demonstrating expected behavior, students identifying key behaviors, and all students practicing).
MM 9 **Participation** Most of the time in our Morning Meetings ...	**1** ... not all students are greeted by class members.	**3** ... each student is greeted and also greets at least one other class member.	**5** ... everyone in the classroom (including all adults, visitors, etc.) is greeted and also greets at least one other person.

SHARING

MM 10 **Appropriateness** Generally, during our Morning Meetings ...	**1** ... *most* students' sharing is focused on games, toys, possessions, or inappropriate personal experiences.	**3** ... *most* students' sharing is focused on appropriate personal experiences, relationships, or ideas and items related to the social or academic curriculum.	**5** ... *all* students' sharing is focused on appropriate personal experiences, relationships, or ideas and items related to the social or academic curriculum.
MM 11 **Appropriateness** During Morning Meeting, students ...	**1** ... *often* share information that may be hurtful or embarrassing to others.	**3** ... *often* share information that is respectful of others and does not lead to hurt feelings.	**5** ... *always or almost always* share information that is respectful of others and does not lead to hurt feelings.

	1	**3**	**5**
MM 12 **Sharing Focus** Generally, during sharing ...	... *few* students' sharings are focused on one main idea with a few supporting details.	... *many* students' sharings are focused on one main idea with a few supporting details.	... *all or almost all* students' sharings are focused on one main idea with a few supporting details.
MM 13 **Speaking Skills** Generally, during sharing ...	... *many* students look down, away, or only at the teacher as they share.	... *many* students look around at all the others in the circle as they share.	... *all or almost all* students look around at all the others in the circle as they share.
MM 14 **Speaking Skills** In general ...	... *many* students who share speak too softly or unclearly to be understood.	... *many* students who share speak loudly and clearly enough to be understood.	... *all or almost all* students who share speak loudly and clearly enough to be understood.
MM 15 **Sharing Length** Generally, during our dialogue sharing ...	... *many* students limit their sharing to one sentence (for example, "I went on a fun trip") or expand their sharing into overly long narrations.	... *some* students provide enough information (that is, several sentences) to give listeners important details, but not so much as to make sharing overly long.	... *many or most* students provide enough information (that is, several sentences) to provide listeners with important details, but not so much as to make sharing overly long.
MM 16 **Questions and Comments** Generally, during dialogue sharing ...	... *no* questions or comments are asked for or given.	... I ask or tell the group to offer questions or comments and/or *some* sharers receive questions or comments.	... *most or all* sharing students tell the group they are ready for questions and comments and all sharing students receive at least two or three questions or comments.

MM 17 **Questions and Comments** The questions and comments students offer are ...	**1** ... *frequently* not respectful of the sharer and/or are off topic.	**3** ... *often* respectful of the sharer and on topic.	**5** ... *almost always* respectful of the sharer and on topic.

GROUP ACTIVITY

MM 18 **Teaching Activities** In general, I ...	**1** ... *do not* usually use Interactive Modeling to teach or remind children about expectations for behavior during the group activity (Interactive Modeling consists of the teacher and one or more students demonstrating expected behavior, students identifying key behaviors, and all students practicing).	**3** ... *sometimes* use Interactive Modeling to teach and review appropriate behavior during the group activity or regularly use portions of Interactive Modeling (Interactive Modeling consists of the teacher and one or more students demonstrating expected behavior, students identifying key behaviors, and all students practicing).	**5** ... *regularly* use Interactive Modeling to teach and review appropriate behavior during the group activity (Interactive Modeling consists of the teacher and one or more students demonstrating expected behavior, students identifying key behaviors, and all students practicing).
MM 19 **Community-Building** In general, the activities I choose encourage ...	**1** ... divisiveness and/or competitiveness in the group. *For example, I choose elimination games.*	**3** ... student cooperation, but students often do not help each other and/or make the activities into a competition.	**5** ... student cooperation and community spirit. *For example, I choose cooperative games in which students help one another.*

MORNING MESSAGE

MM 20 **Preparation** In general, I ...	**1** ... *often do not* write a morning message.	**3** ... *often* write the morning message after students have arrived.	**5** ... *usually* write the morning message before students arrive.

MM 21 **Formatting** The morning message ...	**1** ... is *rarely* written on chart paper or interactive whiteboard and displayed at children's eye level.	**3** ... is *sometimes* written on chart paper or interactive whiteboard and displayed at children's eye level.	**5** ... is *always or almost always* written on chart paper or interactive whiteboard and displayed at children's eye level.
MM 22 **Location** The morning message ...	**1** ... is *not* located in an easily accessible area of the room (that is, where approximately three to five students can get close to the message); instead, it's in a tight corner, behind my desk, etc.	**3** ... is *sometimes* located in an easily accessible area of the room (that is, where approximately three to five students can easily get close to the message).	**5** ... is *regularly* located in an easily accessible area of the room (that is, where approximately three to five students can easily get close to the message).
MM 23 **Readability** Usually, the morning message ...	**1** ... focuses on multiple topics, and may use several words or concepts that several students find difficult.	**3** ... uses vocabulary and academic content familiar to *most* students or focuses primarily on one topic.	**5** ... uses vocabulary and academic content familiar to *all or almost all* students and focuses primarily on one topic.
MM 24 **Interactivity** In general, the morning message ...	**1** ... does not include a component that inspires students to contribute their ideas.	**3** ... inspires students to contribute their ideas but only by writing or drawing on the message.	**5** ... inspires students to contribute their ideas in various ways. *For example, the students can contribute by writing or drawing on the message, considering "thinking questions" that we discuss during the meeting, and/or sharing related ideas during the meeting.*

MM 25 **Engagement** In general, prior to the start of Morning Meeting ...	**1** ... *many* students need a lot of prompting to read the morning message and/or need reminders to follow directions found in the message.	**3** ... *many* students read the morning message with little prompting and follow directions found in the message.	**5** ... *all or almost all* students read the morning message with little prompting and follow directions found in the message.
MM 26 **Usage** In general, during Morning Meeting I ...	**1** ... *rarely* have the whole class read/discuss the morning message as a way to transition to the academic content of the day.	**3** ... *sometimes* have the whole class read/discuss the morning message as a way to transition to the academic content of the day.	**5** ... *always or almost always* have the whole class read/discuss the morning message as a way to transition to the academic content of the day.

Morning Meeting   Total number of points* = _____ divided by 26 items = _____ (average)

Note: Items that you do not rate should be assigned a point value of zero.

Average score _____   **Strength area:**   **Good progress:**   **Area to be improved:**
                          (average: 4.0 or more)   *(average: 3.0–3.9)*   *(average: less than 3.0)*

1. What is an area of particular strength with this practice? What has contributed to your success?

2. What would you identify as areas for improvement?

3. Prioritize these areas for improvement in order of most importance to you.

4. For your first area of priority, create a self-improvement plan (use notes page if needed). See suggestions in the strategies and resources section for specific ideas about ways to work on one or more of the components of this practice.

5. Continue this process with other priority areas.

6. When will you assess this practice again?

NOTES

NOTES

Section 4. Guided Discovery

PRE-ASSESSMENT REFLECTION

I. Reflect on what you currently know about the area of practice you are planning to assess.

II. Thoroughly read through this section of the assessment tool. Note ideas that confirm your best understanding of this practice and ideas that raise questions for you. Think about what the most important goals of this practice are.

III. If you have many questions or potential misunderstandings about this practice, you may want to refer to some of the resources listed in the guide before you assess yourself with the assessment tool.

IV. Complete the section assessment.

Section 4. Guided Discovery ✳ Date assessed _____

GENERAL

GD 1 **Space** In general, during my Guided Discoveries . . .	**1** . . . students are crowded and/or cannot view everyone and everything.	**3** . . . *most* students can sit comfortably in a circle/oval or around a single table and can view everyone and everything.	**5** . . . *all* students can sit comfortably in a circle/oval or at a single table and view everyone and everything.

INTRODUCTION

GD 2 **Key Vocabulary** When the class works with vocabulary, I . . .	**1** . . . do not present or elicit from students key vocabulary related to the material(s).	**3** . . . tell students the common vocabulary words related to the material(s). *For example, if we're studying nonfiction books, I define "table of contents" or "glossary" for them.*	**5** . . . work with students (asking questions, refining answers) to elicit and define a common vocabulary related to the material(s). *For example, if we're studying nonfiction books, I guide them in defining "table of contents" or "glossary" for themselves.*

85

	1	**3**	**5**
GD 3 **Accessing Student Knowledge About Use** To find out students' prior knowledge and experience of the material(s) I'm introducing, I ...	... do not ask questions and/or I just tell students what I want them to know about the material.	... ask mostly closed-ended (such as yes/no) questions. *For example, I might say, "Do we use dictionaries to look up what a word means?"*	... ask mostly open-ended questions. *For example, I might say, "What do you know about dictionaries?"*
GD 4 **Generating Ideas for Use** Generally ...	... students *do not* generate ideas for use of the material(s) and/or ideas for use of the material(s) come primarily from me.	... students generate one or two ideas for use of the material(s).	... students generate at least three or four ideas for use of the material(s).
GD 5 **Student Modeling** Generally ...	... students *do not* model ideas for using the material(s) and/or only I model ideas for using the material(s).	... one student models an idea for using the material(s).	... at least two students model an idea for using the material(s); modeling includes one or more of the student-generated ideas for use or care of the material(s).

	1	**3**	**5**
GD 6 **Task** Generally, the task I specify for the children's exploration …	… does not have clear limits or guidelines. *For example, I might say, "Use the colored pencils to draw a picture" or "Explore different things you can do with the colored pencils."*	… is close-ended. *For example, I might say, "Use the colored pencils to draw a flower just like this one."*	… is open-ended and has clear limits or guidelines. *For example, I might say, "Use the colored pencils to draw different types of circles" or "Use the colored pencils to make lines of different thicknesses and lengths."*
GD 7 **Task** In general, the quantity of materials …	… is too small to enable each student to work with a small set on his or her own.	… is plentiful enough for all, but students work individually or collectively with a large set of the material(s). *For example, students are given the whole box of colored pencils, rather than just one or two.*	… is plentiful enough for all, and each student is given a small set of the material(s) to work with to keep her or him focused on the key properties of the material(s). *For example, students are given one or two colored pencils rather than a whole box.*
GD 8 **Teacher Involvement** In general, I …	… observe the whole class and do not engage with individual students.	… engage with individual students but primarily give help and advice, reinforce positive behavior, and redirect misbehavior.	… engage with individual students by frequently asking open-ended questions and also give help and advice, reinforce positive behavior, and redirect misbehavior. *For example, I might ask, "So why did you decide to use these colors in your drawing?"*

	1	**3**	**5**
GD 9 **Process** In general, I . . .	. . . allow an *extended* amount of time and negotiation to determine who will share and the order in which they will share.	. . . allow a *moderate* amount of time and negotiation to determine who will share and the order in which they will share.	. . . *quickly* determine who will share and the order in which they will share.
GD 10 **Content** In general, . . .	. . . I determine which students will share.	. . . everyone in the group who wants to share has a chance to do so.	. . . I call on two to six volunteers; students who do not wish to share are not required to do so.
GD 11 **Content** In general, I . . .	. . . do not structure the sharing. *For example, I'll simply instruct students to "share what you worked on."*	. . . structure the sharing by asking students to respond to specific prompts. *For example, I might say, "Tell us why you used the color red in your work."*	. . . . use an open-ended question to structure the sharing for all sharers. *For example, I might ask, "What is one thing that you like about your work?"*
GD 12 **Speaking Skills** In general, . . .	. . . . *many* students who share look away from other students and adults or look only at the teacher.	. . . *many* students who share look at all the other students and adults in the group.	. . . *all or almost all* students who share look at all the other students and adults in the group.
GD 13 **Speaking Skills** In general, . . .	. . . *many* students who share speak too softly or unclearly to be understood and/or sit or stand so that other people in the group cannot easily see them.	. . . *many* students who share speak loudly and clearly enough to be understood and stand or sit so other people in the group can easily see them.	. . . *all or almost all* students who share speak loudly and clearly enough to be understood and stand or sit so other people in the group can easily see them.

	1	**3**	**5**
GD 14 **Interactive Modeling** In general, before the whole class cleans up . . .	. . . students *do not* model cleaning up and putting away material(s).	. . . one or two students *do* model how to put away the materials but students do not name key behaviors. *For example, a student models putting a book back on the shelf, but others do not comment that she's putting the book so that the spine faces out, the book is right-side up, etc.*	. . . one or two students *do* model how to put away the materials and other students name key behaviors. *For example, a student models putting a book back on the shelf, and others comment that she's putting the book so that the spine faces out, the book is right-side up, etc.*
GD 15 **Procedure** During cleanup . . .	. . . I or *a few* designated students store materials in the appropriate classroom locations.	. . . *some* students independently store materials in the appropriate classroom locations and I or *a few* designated students store materials for other students.	. . . *most* students independently store materials in the appropriate classroom locations. *For example, students put dictionaries in the reading corner bookcase on a shelf that is within easy reach of all the children.*

Guided Discovery   Total number of points* = _____ divided by 15 items = _____ (average)

*Note: Items that you do not rate should be assigned a point value of zero.

POST-ASSESSMENT REFLECTION

Average score _____   **Strength area:**   **Good progress:**   **Area to be improved:**

(average: 4.0 or more)   (average: 3.0–3.9)   (average: less than 3.0)

1. What is an area of particular strength with this practice? What has contributed to your success?

2. What would you identify as areas for improvement?

3. Prioritize these areas for improvement in order of most importance to you.

4. For your first area of priority, create a self-improvement plan (use notes page if needed). See suggestions in the strategies and resources section for specific ideas about ways to work on one or more of the components of this practice.

5. Continue this process with other priority areas.

6. When will you assess this practice again?

NOTES

Section 5. Academic Choice

PRE-ASSESSMENT REFLECTION

I. Reflect on what you currently know about the area of practice you are planning to assess.

II. Thoroughly read through this section of the assessment tool. Note ideas that confirm your best understanding of this practice and ideas that raise questions for you. Think about what the most important goals of this practice are.

III. If you have many questions or potential misunderstandings about this practice, you may want to refer to some of the resources listed in the guide before you assess yourself with the assessment tool.

IV. Complete the section assessment.

Section 5. Academic Choice ✳ Date assessed _____

INTRODUCTION & PLANNING PHASE

	1	**3**	**5**
AC 1 **Learning Goal** The learning goal of Academic Choice is . . .	. . . *often* not clearly stated for students.	. . . *sometimes* clearly stated for students.	. . . *usually* clearly stated for students.
	1	**3**	**5**
AC 2 **Learning Goal** The learning goal of Academic Choice is . . .	. . . *often* not part of our class's regular curriculum; instead, I offer choice only during special enrichment and holiday activities, or during activities to keep children occupied at arrival, indoor recess, dismissal time, etc.	. . . *sometimes* part of our class's regular curriculum.	. . . *often* part of our class's regular curriculum. *For example, if we're studying marine biology, students choose an animal to research and choose how to show what they've learned.*

AC 3 **Characteristics of Choices** Students often can choose ...	**1** ... only with whom to work, where to work, or when to do work.	**3** ... only among *closed-ended* choices about what kind of work to do, how to do the work, or both. *For example, I offer choices among worksheets or other tasks with only one or two correct outcomes.*	**5** ... among *open-ended* choices about what kind of work to do, how to do the work, or both. *For example, I allow students to choose an animal to learn about or to choose how to show what they learned about an assigned animal, or to choose both what animal to study and how to show what they learned.*
AC 4 **Number of Choices Provided** I often give students ...	**1** ... more than six choices.	**3** ... either two or more than six choices.	**5** ... between three and six choices.
AC 5 **Processes** When students are making their choices ...	**1** ... an *extended* amount of negotiation, long deliberation, or complaining often occurs.	**3** ... a *moderate* amount of negotiation, long deliberation, or complaining often occurs.	**5** ... *most* students make decisions with *little or no* negotiation, long deliberation, or complaining.
AC 6 **Materials** The materials students use ...	**1** ... must be handed out by a teacher or designated student helper.	**3** ... can sometimes be easily accessed independently by students.	**5** ... can *usually* be easily accessed independently by students.
AC 7 **Materials** The materials students use ...	**1** ... are often ones that students *do not* have prior experience using in my classroom through Interactive Modeling and practice or Guided Discovery.	**3** ... are often, but not always, ones that students *do* have prior experience using in my classroom through Interactive Modeling and practice or Guided Discovery.	**5** ... are always or almost always ones that students do have prior experience using in my classroom through Interactive Modeling and practice or Guided Discovery.

	1	**3**	**5**
AC 8 **Teacher Facilitation** Usually, I . . .	. . . name or list the choices but *do not* provide examples or help students generate ideas for what they might do or materials they might use for any of the choices.	. . . provide examples or help students generate ideas for what they might do or materials they might use for *some* of the choices.	. . . provide examples or help students generate ideas for what they might do or materials they might use for all or almost all the choices. *For example, I might show students a picture book, a poster, and a model, all depicting something about seals.*
AC 9 **Teacher Facilitation** Usually, I . . .	. . . *do not* record the choices students make.	. . . *do* record the choices students make in a notebook that I keep.	. . . *do* record the choices students make or have students record their choices on a public sign-up sheet or board or a student planning sheet.

TRANSITION FROM PLANNING PHASE TO WORKING PHASE

	1	**3**	**5**
AC 10 **Teacher Facilitation** During the transition between planning and working phases, I usually . . .	. . . focus on preparation for the working phase by directing students, setting up materials, and handing out supplies.	. . . engage with individual students to be sure they know what they are supposed to be doing as they prepare to work on chosen activities.	. . . take time to observe and provide feedback to the whole class as they independently prepare to work on chosen activities.
AC 11 **Teacher Facilitation** During the transition between planning and working phases, I usually . . .	. . . tell students it is time to go to work and they immediately transition to the working phase with no discussion.	. . . briefly give directions or review expectations for the working phase and then dismiss students to begin work.	. . . briefly give directions or review expectations for the working phase and then call on volunteers to name the key ideas of these directions or expectations before dismissing students to work.

AC 12 **Teacher Facilitation** Usually, while students are working on their choices, I . . .	**1** . . . observe the whole class or work on teacher tasks and do not engage with individual students.	**3** . . . engage with individual students but *do not* frequently use open-ended questions or reinforcing language. *For example, I might say, "I like/notice how you drew your seal" or ask, "Did you learn that seals have fat to keep them warm?"*	**5** . . . engage with individual students and use many open-ended questions and reinforcing language to foster their thinking and curiosity and ensure they're meeting the learning goal. *For example, I might ask, "What are you learning about the seal?" or "What is interesting to you about this?" or I might say, "I see you're showing lots of ways seals defend themselves."*
AC 13 **Work Space** The spaces where students work are . . .	**1** . . . *mostly not* comfortable or conducive to work.	**3** . . . *somewhat* comfortable and conducive to work.	**5** . . . *mostly* comfortable and conducive to work.

S H A R I N G   &   R E F L E C T I N G   P H A S E

AC 14 **Meeting Space** Usually, when we reflect as a group . . .	**1** . . . *few* students are able to sit comfortably in a circle and view everyone and everything.	**3** . . . *most* students are able to sit comfortably in a circle and view everyone and everything.	**5** . . . *all* students are able to sit comfortably in a circle and view everyone and everything.
AC 15 **Content** Usually, when students share their work . . .	**1** . . . I designate which students will share.	**3** . . . sharing is voluntary, but all or most students share their work; students who do not wish to share are not required to do so.	**5** . . . sharing is voluntary, and only two to six students share at any one meeting; students who do not wish to share are not required to do so.

	1	**3**	**5**
AC 16 **Content** Usually, when students reflect on their work, I ...	... do not use open-ended "focus questions" to structure the reflecting; instead, I simply ask students to "share your work" or ask a specific question, such as, "Why did you use the color red in your work?"	... structure students' reflecting by providing a broad, open-ended "focus question," such as, "Tell one thing that you like about your work," but I allow students to choose whether to respond to the question or to decide for themselves what they will say.	... structure students' reflecting by expecting all students to respond to a broad, open-ended "focus question," such as, "What's one thing you like about your work?"
AC 17 **Student Self-Reflection** Usually, at the end of Academic Choice ...	... we skip the reflecting phase because we have no time for it.	... students reflect on their work by assigning themselves grades or comparing their work with that of their classmates.	... I pose open-ended "focus questions" or provide a rubric for students to use as they reflect on their work and their learning.
AC 18 **Student Self-Reflection** Usually, at the end of Academic Choice, I ...	... *always* assign grades to students' choice work.	... *sometimes* assign grades to students' choice work.	... *rarely* assign grades to students' choice work.

Academic Choice   Total number of points* = _____ divided by 18 items = _____ (average)

Note: Items that you do not rate should be assigned a point value of zero.

Average score _____ **Strength area:**   **Good progress:**   **Area to be improved:**
                         (average: 4.0 or more)   *(average: 3.0–3.9)*   *(average: less than 3.0)*

1. What is an area of particular strength with this practice? What has contributed to your success?

2. What would you identify as areas for improvement?

3. Prioritize these areas for improvement in order of most importance to you.

4. For your first area of priority, create a self-improvement plan (use notes page if needed).
    See suggestions in the strategies and resources section for specific ideas about ways to work
    on one or more of the components of this practice.

5. Continue this process with other priority areas.

6. When will you assess this practice again?

NOTES

Section 6. Classroom Organization

P R E - A S S E S S M E N T   R E F L E C T I O N

I. Reflect on what you currently know about the area of practice you are planning to assess.

II. Thoroughly read through this section of the assessment tool. Note ideas that confirm your best understanding of this practice and ideas that raise questions for you. Think about what the most important goals of this practice are.

III. If you have many questions or potential misunderstandings about this practice, you may want to refer to some of the resources listed in the guide before you assess yourself with the assessment tool.

IV. Complete the section assessment.

Section 6. Classroom Organization ✳ Date assessed _____

	1	**3**	**5**
CO 1 **Classroom Space** My classroom is . . .	. . . dirty, disorganized, and/or cluttered.	. . . *somewhat* clean, organized, and free of clutter.	. . . *mostly* clean, organized, and free of clutter.
CO 2 **Furniture Arrangement** Furniture is arranged so that . . .	. . . *most* walkways and gathering places are crowded and sometimes uncomfortable for students.	. . . *some* walkways and gathering places are crowded or uncomfortable but some have adequate space so that students are comfortable.	. . . *all* main walkways and gathering places have enough space for students to line up safely and comfortably and passageways in the room are large enough for two children to pass safely.
CO 3 **Visibility of Students** I can see students . . .	. . . from a *few* places in the classroom.	. . . from *many* places in the classroom.	. . . from *any or almost any* place in the classroom.

	1	**3**	**5**
CO 4 **Work Spaces** Students primarily work . . .	. . . at desks arranged in rows or a U shape.	. . . at desks arranged in clusters or at tables with other students.	. . . in various seating arrangements depending on their developmental and individual needs: whole group, small group, and individual.
CO 5 **Storage of Classroom Materials** My classroom materials are . . .	. . . disorganized and not accessible for students.	. . . *either* well-organized or accessible for students to gather and put away independently.	. . . *both* well-organized and accessible for students to gather and put away independently.
CO 6 **Displays & Wall Decorations:** **Content** My classroom displays are . . .	. . . *mostly* store-bought and/or teacher-made borders, displays, or posters.	. . . *a mix* of store-bought and/or teacher-made borders, displays, or posters along with some examples of student work.	. . . *mostly* student work and include examples of work from all the students in my class.
CO 7 **Displays & Wall Decorations:** **Presentation** Classroom rules and other displays and decorations are . . .	. . . *mostly* hanging partially off the walls.	. . . *mostly* neatly secured to a wall.	. . . *all* neatly secured to a wall.
CO 8 **Displays & Wall Decorations:** **Presentation** Classroom rules and other displays and decorations are . . .	. . . *not* labeled with titles or captions.	. . . *sometimes* clearly marked with titles or captions.	. . . *always or nearly always* clearly marked with titles or captions.

	1	**3**	**5**
CO 9 **Displays & Wall Decorations: Presentation** Classroom rules and other displays and decorations . . .	. . . are crowded together.	. . . *sometimes* have ample blank or "white" space between them.	. . . *always or nearly always* have ample blank or "white" space between them.
CO 10 **Displays & Wall Decorations: Presentation** Classroom rules and other displays and decorations are . . .	. . . *often* above students' eye level.	. . . *sometimes* at students' eye level.	. . . *always or nearly always* at students' eye level.
CO 11 **Time-Out Place** My classroom has . . .	. . . no pre-designated time-out place or the time-out place is outside the classroom.	. . . a pre-designated time-out place in a high-traffic area or near a door to the hallway.	. . . a pre-designated time-out place in an out-of-the-way area inside the classroom.
CO 12 **Visibility of Time-Out Place** My classroom has . . .	. . . no pre-designated time-out place or a place in which I *sometimes* cannot see the child.	. . . a pre-designated time-out place in which I *often* can see the child.	. . . a pre-designated time-out place in which I *always or almost always* can see the child.

Classroom Organization Total number of points* = _____ divided by 12 items = _____ (average)

Note: Items that you do not rate should be assigned a point value of zero.

POST-ASSESSMENT REFLECTION

Average score _____   **Strength area:**   **Good progress:**   **Area to be improved:**
                            (average: 4.0 or more)   (average: 3.0–3.9)   (average: less than 3.0)

1. What is an area of particular strength with this practice? What has contributed to your success?

2. What would you identify as areas for improvement?

3. Prioritize these areas for improvement in order of most importance to you.

4. For your first area of priority, create a self-improvement plan (use notes page if needed). See suggestions in the strategies and resources section for specific ideas about ways to work on one or more of the components of this practice.

5. Continue this process with other priority areas.

6. When will you assess this practice again?

NOTES

Section 7. Classroom Management and Teacher Language

I. Reflect on what you currently know about the area of practice you are planning to assess.

II. Thoroughly read through this section of the assessment tool. Note ideas that confirm your best understanding of this practice and ideas that raise questions for you. Think about what the most important goals of this practice are.

III. If you have many questions or potential misunderstandings about this practice, you may want to refer to some of the resources listed in the guide before you assess yourself with the assessment tool.

IV. Complete the section assessment.

Section 7. Classroom Management and Teacher Language ✳ Date assessed _____

CLASSROOM RULES

	1	3	5
CM 1 **Creation: Who** In my classroom …	… I create the classroom rules or use preestablished rules and tell students my expectations.	… the students and I create and/or discuss the classroom rules together.	… the students and I create and/or discuss the classroom rules together and the printed rules incorporate students' words and other input such as signatures or decorations.
CM 2 **Creation: Who** In my classroom, I …	… *do not* have students think about and share their hopes and dreams for the year before establishing classroom rules.	… *do* have students think about and share their hopes and dreams for the year but do not tie hopes and dreams to the rules.	… *do* have students think about and share their hopes and dreams for the year and do tie their hopes and dreams to the rules.
CM 3 **Number** Our classroom has …	… no classroom rules.	… fewer than three or more than five classroom rules.	… between three and five classroom rules.

CM 4 **Presentation** My classroom rules are …	**1** … not written and posted.	**3** … written and posted but are not attractively posted and/or are not at the children's eye level.	**5** … written and attractively posted at the children's eye level.
CM 5 **Content** Our classroom rules are …	**1** … mostly stated as what *not* to do. *For example, "Do not be rude," rather than "Be kind to others."*	**3** … somewhat or mostly stated as what *to* do. *For example, "Be kind to others," rather than "Do not be rude."*	**5** … all stated as what *to* do. *For example, "Be kind to others," rather than "Do not be rude."*

S I G N A L S

CM 6 **Using Signals** Usually, when I need students' attention, I …	**1** … raise my voice or tell children "shhh."	**3** … *sometimes* use a predictable signal to gain the attention of my class but sometimes raise my voice or tell children "shhh."	**5** … *consistently* use a predictable signal to gain the attention of my class throughout the day. *For example, every time I want to gain the class's attention, I raise my hand, clap, use a chime, etc.*
CM 7 **Student Response to Signals** When using a signal, I …	**1** … begin to speak when *few* students are quiet, have eyes on me, and are keeping hands and legs to themselves.	**3** … begin to speak when *many* students are quiet, have eyes on me, and are keeping hands and legs to themselves.	**5** … begin to speak when *all* students are quiet, have eyes on me, and are keeping hands and legs to themselves.

CM 8 **Teaching Signals to Students** Before expecting students to follow signals, I …	**1** … do not teach students my expectations for responding to signals.	**3** … tell and personally demonstrate how I expect students to respond to signals.	**5** … teach how I expect students to respond to signals through Interactive Modeling and practice.
CM 9 **When Students Don't Meet Expectations for Signals** When students do not meet my expectations for responding to signals, I …	**1** … *do not* use Interactive Modeling and practice to review expectations.	**3** … *sometimes* use Interactive Modeling and practice to review expectations.	**5** … *often* use Interactive Modeling and practice to review expectations.

BEGINNING LESSONS & ACTIVITIES

CM 10 **Student Readiness** I begin lessons when …	**1** … *many* students are distracted and/or talking.	**3** … *many* students are quiet, have still bodies, are keeping hands and legs to themselves, and are looking at me.	**5** … *all or almost all* students are quiet, have still bodies, are keeping hands and legs to themselves, and are looking at me.

TRANSITIONS

CM 11 **Before** Before transition time, I …	**1** … *do not* review expectations for the next activity.	**3** … tell students directions for the next activity.	**5** … briefly give directions and review expectations and then call on volunteers to name key ideas of directions and expectations before dismissing students to begin the next activity.

CM 12 **During** During transition time, I . . .	**1** . . . am busy preparing for the next activity or consulting with colleagues.	**3** . . . focus on helping a few students as they change activities.	**5** . . . do not often engage with individual students or focus on preparation for the next activity but do observe the whole class as they change activities with independence.

T E A C H E R   L A N G U A G E

CM 13 **Tone and Rate of Speech** When talking to students, I . . .	**1** . . . *often* speak with a raised, angry, pleading, or rushed voice.	**3** . . . *sometimes* speak with a raised, angry, pleading, or rushed voice.	**5** . . . *typically* speak with a calm and respectful voice.
CM 14 **Voiceovers** When students respond to my questions or offer comments, before I speak further or call on another student, I . . .	**1** . . . *often* repeat all or part of what the student said. *For example, a student responds, "All mammals have fur," and I respond, "Yes, fur. What else do all mammals have?"*	**3** . . . *sometimes* respond to the student's comment or call on another student but *sometimes* repeat all or part of what the student said.	**5** . . . *typically* pause a moment and then respond to the student's comment or call on another student but *do not* repeat student's comments back to him/her. *For example, a student responds, "All mammals have fur," and I nod. Then I ask, "What else do all mammals have?"*
CM 15 **Reinforcing** When I am reinforcing a student who is behaving appropriately, I will typically . . .	**1** . . . express general approval. *For example, I might say, "Good job, Marisa" or "Nice drawing."*	**3** . . . express approval for concrete and specific behaviors. *For example, I might say, "I like how lots of people pushed in their chairs" or "Marisa, good job cleaning up your materials faster today."*	**5** . . . describe concrete and specific behaviors. *For example, I might say, "I see lots of people who remembered to push in their chairs" or "Marisa, I notice that you cleaned up your materials faster today."*

	1	3	5
CM 16 **Reminding** When students need reminders about expectations for behavior, I …	… *usually* re-explain the expectations for them. *For example, I might say, "Don't forget to pack your homework" or "You should stop running."*	… *sometimes* ask a question or make a statement that invites them to remember and demonstrate the expected behavior.	… *often* ask a question or make a statement that invites them to remember and demonstrate the expected behavior. *For example, I might say, "What do you need to be doing right now?" or "Show me how you will follow our rules."*
CM 17 **Reminding** Usually, I use reminding or redirecting language when I am …	… angry or upset and students are out of control or upset.	… still calm but sometimes students are out of control or upset.	… still calm and students are not yet out of control or upset.
CM 18 **Redirecting** When redirecting students, I …	… *often* phrase the command as a question. *For example, I might ask, "Mario, do you want me to take those toys away?" or "Sonya, would you sit down, please?"*	… *sometimes* give brief directions in the form of a statement but *sometimes* phrase the command as a question.	… *typically* give brief and nonnegotiable directions in the form of a statement. *For example, I might say, "Mario, hands in your lap" or "Sonya, walk."*
CM 19 **Redirecting** When redirecting students, I …	… *often* name what they should *not* be doing. *For example, I might say, "Sonya, stop running."*	… *sometimes* name what I want them to do but sometimes name what they should not be doing.	… *usually* name what I want them to do. *For example, I might say, "Sonya, walk."*

CM 20 Redirecting When redirecting students, I am …	**1** … *often* angry or upset.	**3** … *often* calm but sometimes don't intervene until the students are out of control or upset.	**5** … *usually* calm and intervene before students are out of control or upset.
CM 21 Language Frequency I spend …	**1** … *more time* on general praise, reminders, and redirections than on reinforcing language.	**3** … *about the same amount of time* on reinforcing language as on general praise, reminders, and redirections.	**5** … *more time* on reinforcing language than on general praise, reminders, and redirections.

LOGICAL CONSEQUENCES

CM 22 Respectful Tone When I respond to students' misbehavior, my tone of voice is …	**1** … *often* yelling, pleading, blaming, or sarcastic.	**3** … *sometimes* calm and respectful, but *sometimes* yelling, pleading, blaming, or sarcastic.	**5** … *usually* calm and respectful.
CM 23 Relevant The consequences I use in my classroom are …	**1** … *often* predetermined. *For example, I have charts of increasingly severe consequences based on numbers of tallied misbehaviors or lists of consequences for certain misbehaviors, such as "No homework = no recess."*	**3** … *not* predetermined but often unrelated to the misbehavior or its context. *For example, I usually use loss of recess or time-out for not doing homework regardless of individual circumstances.*	**5** … *not* predetermined and also related to what will help the particular student calm down and/or repair damage resulting from the misbehavior. *For example, a student who draws on a desk may clean the desk, move to another location to work for awhile, or take a time-out, depending on what will most help the particular student change the behavior.*

	1	**3**	**5**
CM 24 **Realistic** The consequences I use in my classroom are …	… *generally* overly severe and/or difficult for me to enforce. *For example, a student who draws on his or her own desk cleans all desks.*	… *sometimes* overly severe and difficult for me to enforce but sometimes reasonable for the student to do and for me to enforce.	… *generally* reasonable for the student to do and for me to enforce. *For example, a student who draws on his or her own desk cleans his or her own desk.*
CM 25 **Negotiation of Logical Consequences** At the moment when I need to give a logical consequence, I …	… *often* negotiate with students and/or offer a lengthy explanation about the reason for the consequence.	… *sometimes* negotiate with students and/or engage in conversation about the reason for the consequence.	… do *not* negotiate consequences with students or engage in conversation about the reason for the consequence. *For example, I stop students when they try to explain their actions, ask questions about a consequence, or bargain down their consequences.*
CM 26 **Introduction of Logical Consequences** In the first weeks of school, after we create rules, I …	… tell the children about the types of consequences I will use for misbehavior and/or post a list of consequences.	… introduce logical consequences by naming the three types and/or showing children how to go to time-out.	… introduce logical consequences by discussing ways that we all break the rules and need help following them sometimes. Then I teach children how to go to time-out.
CM 27 **Expectations for Time-Out** In the first weeks of school, I teach my expectations for going to and returning from time-out by …	… explaining the expected behaviors, showing where to go, and explaining how to come back.	… explaining and demonstrating the expected behaviors one or more times.	… using Interactive Modeling and opportunities for each child to practice the expected behaviors.

	1	**3**	**5**	
CM 28 **Purpose of Time-Out** I teach students that time-out is a place for . . .	. . . punishing bad behavior.	. . . thinking about what they did wrong.	. . . relaxing and feeling more in control.	

	1	**3**	**5**	
CM 29 **Going to Time-Out** When directing students to time-out, I . . .	. . . *do not* use a brief and clear command. *For example, I might say "Tim, will you please go to time-out?" or "Tim, that's enough of that! Now you have to take a break."*	. . . *sometimes* use a brief and clear command.	. . . *consistently* use a brief and clear command. *For example, I might say, "Tim, take a break."*	

	1	**3**	**5**	
CM 30 **Going to Time-Out** When students typically go to time-out . . .	. . . *few* students go immediately and quietly.	. . . *many* students go immediately and quietly.	. . . *all or almost all* students go immediately and quietly.	

	1	**3**	**5**	**(N/A)**
CM 31 **Going to Time-Out** When students who must go to time-out attempt to stall, argue, or create disruptions, I . . .	. . . *often* engage with the students by negotiating or arguing with them, or ignore them or try to stop the behavior by lecturing, embarrassing, or using punishments, such as sending them to the principal.	. . . *sometimes* ignore or punish the students but *sometimes* call for a buddy teacher.	. . . *usually* call for a buddy teacher and have the students removed from the classroom until they are calm.	No students ever attempt to stall, argue, or create disruptions when they must go to time-out.

CM 32 **During Time-Out** Typically, students in time-out …	**1** … are disruptive and/or work on tasks. *For example, students talk or bang hands or feet and/or bring classwork or writing of a disciplinary nature, such as a plan for better behavior.*	**3** … sit quietly and calmly or do not work on any tasks.	**5** … sit quietly and calmly and do not work on any tasks. *For example, students do not talk or bang with hands or feet and do not bring classwork or writing of a disciplinary nature, such as a plan for better behavior.*	
CM 33 **During Time-Out** Typically, if students continue misbehaving while in time-out, I …	**1** … *often* give them reminders or redirections.	**3** … *sometimes* give them reminders or redirections.	**5** … *do not* give them reminders or redirections. Instead, I call for a buddy teacher if needed.	**(N/A)** No students ever misbehave while in time-out.
CM 34 **Leaving Time-Out** When students leave time-out …	**1** … their behavior often continues to be disruptive and classroom activities are interrupted as they return. *For example, the student is still angry and I scold the student for pulling books from a bookshelf while returning to her or his seat.*	**3** … they are calm but classroom activities are briefly interrupted as they return. *For example, classmates talk to the student or I ask the student if she or he is ready to return.*	**5** … they are calm and re-enter classroom activities without interruption. *For example, the student rejoins classroom activity without drawing the teacher's or class's attention away from ongoing work.*	
CM 35 **Teacher-Student Discussion** I have a discussion with students about the reason they went to time-out and talk to them about expected behaviors …	**1** … when students are in time-out or before they go to time-out.	**3** … immediately following time-out.	**5** … if needed, later in the day when we are both calm.	

CM 36 **Reason for Time-Out** In general, students are ...	**1** ... *rarely* certain why they went to time-out, and discussion is *often* needed.	**3** ... *sometimes* certain why they went to time-out, and discussion is *sometimes* needed.	**5** ... nearly *always certain* why they went to time-out, and discussion is *rarely* needed.
CM 37 **Buddy Teacher** When students are unable to manage their behavior in our classroom, I ...	**1** ... *do not* have buddy teachers to whom I can send them.	**3** ... *do* have teachers to whom I can send them but the teachers differ depending on the day and other situations.	**5** ... *do* have one or two buddy teachers to whom I can send them and can consistently send them to these same teachers.
CM 38 **Sending Student to Buddy Teacher** When a student is going to the buddy teacher ...	**1** ... another student escorts the student to the buddy teacher's classroom or the student goes to the buddy teacher's classroom unescorted.	**3** ... I send the student to the buddy teacher's classroom and observe the student as he or she walks to the buddy teacher's classroom.	**5** ... the buddy teacher comes to my classroom to remove the student.
CM 39 **Student Returning from Buddy Teacher** When it's time for a student to return from the buddy teacher ...	**1** ... the buddy teacher sends the student back to our classroom.	**3** ... after an established period of time (for example, five minutes), I retrieve the student from the buddy teacher's room.	**5** ... I personally check in with the student in the buddy teacher's room to gauge whether the student is ready to return.

**Classroom Management
and Teacher Language**

Total number of points* = _____ divided by 39 items = _____ (average)

* Note: Items that you do not rate should be assigned a point value of zero. Not applicable ratings (if used for CM 31 or CM 33) should not be calculated into the average.

Average score _____   **Strength area:**   **Good progress:**   **Area to be improved:**
                          (average: 4.0 or more)   *(average: 3.0–3.9)*   *(average: less than 3.0)*

1. What is an area of particular strength with this practice? What has contributed to your success?

2. What would you identify as areas for improvement?

3. Prioritize these areas for improvement in order of most importance to you.

4. For your first area of priority, create a self-improvement plan (use notes page if needed). See suggestions in the strategies and resources section for specific ideas about ways to work on one or more of the components of this practice.

5. Continue this process with other priority areas.

6. When will you assess this practice again?

Section 8. Working With Families

P R E - A S S E S S M E N T   R E F L E C T I O N

I. Reflect on what you currently know about the area of practice you are planning to assess.

II. Thoroughly read through this section of the assessment tool. Note ideas that confirm your best understanding of this practice and ideas that raise questions for you. Think about what the most important goals of this practice are.

III. If you have many questions or potential misunderstandings about this practice, you may want to refer to some of the resources listed in the guide before you assess yourself with the assessment tool.

IV. Complete the section assessment.

Section 8. Working With Families ✳ Date assessed _____

	1	**3**	**5**
WF 1 **Welcoming and Valuing Families** At the beginning of each school year, I ...	... *send a general letter* introducing myself and telling all families about the activities I have planned for their children or *do not* communicate with families at the beginning of the year.	... *send a general letter* telling all families I'm excited to have their children as students and am looking forward to working with them and their children throughout the year.	... *individually talk* to as many individual families as possible and tell each family I'm excited to have their child as a student and am looking forward to working with them and their child throughout the year.
WF 2 **Families as Active Participants** With respect to family participation, I ...	... rarely encourage families to participate; I might occasionally invite those I happen to meet to visit the classroom or ask them questions about their child.	... through *general* communication (such as newsletter and welcome letter), tell as many families as possible what we're doing in the classroom and ask for their opinions on such things as their hopes and dreams for their child.	... through *individual* communication (such as in parent-teacher conferences), tell as many families as possible what we're doing in the classroom and ask for their opinions on such things as their hopes and dreams for their child.

	1	3	5
WF 3 **Communicating With Families** I typically communicate with …	… only those families whose child is having problems in my classroom.	… *some* families throughout the year and *much* of my communication is positive news. *For example, I might say, "Mario is writing such exciting stories" rather than "Mario had trouble staying on task today."*	… *all* families throughout the year, and *much* of my communication is positive news. *For example, I might say "Mario is writing such exciting stories" rather than "Mario had trouble staying on task today."*
WF 4 **Sharing Information and Children's Work** Throughout the school year, I …	… *rarely* share with *any* families information about my classroom practices and their children's work.	… *sometimes* share with *all* families information about my classroom practices and their children's work.	… *routinely* share with *all* families information about my classroom practices and their children's work.
WF 5 **Problem-Solving With Families** When severe academic or behavioral challenges arise and I need to communicate with a family, I …	… *always tell* the family what I have determined the solution to be.	… *sometimes* problem-solve with the family to find a solution we're all comfortable with but sometimes tell the family what I have determined the solution to be.	… *always* problem-solve with the family to find a solution we're all comfortable with.

Working With Families   Total number of points* = _____ divided by 5 items = _____ (average)

Note: Items that you do not rate should be assigned a point value of zero.

Average score _____   **Strength area:**   **Good progress:**   **Area to be improved:**

                      (average: 4.0 or more)   *(average: 3.0–3.9)*   *(average: less than 3.0)*

1. What is an area of particular strength with this practice? What has contributed to your success?

2. What would you identify as areas for improvement?

3. Prioritize these areas for improvement in order of most importance to you.

4. For your first area of priority, create a self-improvement plan (use notes page if needed). See suggestions in the strategies and resources section for specific ideas about ways to work on one or more of the components of this practice.

5. Continue this process with other priority areas.

6. When will you assess this practice again?

NOTES

Responsive Classroom Assessment

	Strength Area (average: 4.0 or more)	Good Progress (average: 3.0–3.9)	Area To Be Improved (average: less than 3.0)
Section 1 Arrival Time			
Section 2 Interactive Modeling			
Section 3 Morning Meeting			
Section 4 Guided Discovery			
Section 5 Academic Choice			
Section 6 Classroom Organization			
Section 7 Classroom Management and Teacher Language			
Section 8 Working With Families			